# COMPLET

# PRACTICE TES

# 2024-2025

# 4 STANDARD & 1 FULL-LENGTH TEST WITH OVER 300 QUESTIONS & ANSWERS

# Anthony R. Rogers

Published by: Galicia Publishing House

Support@BarberryBooks.com

Design & Cover by Rebecca Nickerson

First Edition

# Contents

# Introduction

The Project Management Professional or PMP certification exam helps you get a job as a project manager, leading and directing teams and projects. The PMP certification exam is developed and maintained by the Project Management Institute (PMI) and is designed to have applicants demonstrate their experience in project management. Let's take a brief moment to look at the exam itself; then, we're going to focus the bulk of this book on providing you with the practice tests you need to help you prepare to pass the PMP exam.

# Certification Requirements

To be eligible for the PMP exam, you need to meet the necessary requirements that are based on your level of education.

## Four-Year College Degree

With a college degree, you need at least 36 months of experience leading projects within the last eight years. You also need at least 35 hours of project management education or CAPM certification.

## High School or Secondary School Diploma

With a diploma, you need to have at least 60 months of experience in leading projects within the last eight years. You also need at least 35 hours of project management education or CAPM certification.

# Exam Outline

The PMP exam consists of 180 questions. Five questions are unscored and used to validate questions for future versions of the test. You have 3 hours and 50 minutes to complete the test. The exam consists of three content domains.

# People - 42% of the exam content

The questions within this domain cover the following topics:

- Conflict management

- Team leadership

- Supporting team performance

- Empowering stakeholders and team members

- Ensuring adequate training of team members

- Team building

- Addressing and removing impediments, obstacles and blocks for the team

- Negotiating project agreements

- Collaborating with stakeholders

- Building a shared understanding

- Supporting and engaging virtual teams

- Defining ground rules for teams

- Mentoring of relevant stakeholders

- Applying emotional intelligence to help promote team performance

## Process - 50% of the exam content

The questions within this domain cover the following topics:

- Urgently executing projects required to deliver business value

- Communications management

- Assessing and managing risks

- Engaging stakeholders

- Planning and managing resources and budgets

- Planning and managing schedules

- Planning and managing quality products and/or deliverables

- Planning and managing scope

- Integrating project planning activities

- Managing changes to a project

- Planning and managing procurement

- Managing project artifacts

- Determining appropriate methodology and practice for projects

- Establishing a governance structure for projects

- Managing issues with projects

- Ensuring project continuity with knowledge transfer

- Planning and managing project closure

# Business Environment - 8% of the exam content

The questions within this domain cover the following topics:

- Planning and managing project compliance

- Evaluating and delivering the benefits and value of a project

- Evaluating and addressing the impact on scope from external business environment changes

- Supporting organizational change

# Exam Registration

To register for the PMP exam, you must submit an application through the Project Management Institute (PMI) website. The application needs to include proof of eligibility and a $575 exam fee. PMI members have a discounted exam fee of $405. Once the application is approved and registration processed, you will receive a confirmation email and information on scheduling your exam appointment.

# Taking the Test

It is best to arrive at the test site 15-30 minutes before your exam time. This gives you the time needed to complete the check-in process and relax. When you sign in, you must present a photo ID to the proctor. The proctor will take your photograph and ask you to sign a roster along with other rule forms. Personal items aren't allowed in the testing room, so you should leave them at home, or you'll be asked to place them in a secure locker located outside of the testing area. Before the exam starts, you'll receive a brief tutorial on how the testing system works, and you'll have to sign an NDA.

# Exam Scoring

The PMP certification exam is calculated and scored using the criterion-based scoring system. This means that a panel of experts in the subject-matter evaluates the questions and determines a passing score. PMI doesn't release a minimum passing score requirement, but it is believed that you have to answer at least 70% correctly in order to pass the exam. Before you leave the testing center, you'll receive a preliminary score report, and then, within ten business days, you should receive an official confirmation of your scores.

## Retaking the Exam

If you don't pass the PMP exam, you are allowed to retake it up to two times within a year of your first attempt.

Now that we know more about the exam itself, it's time to help you get prepared to take the test. The bulk of this book is going to provide you with practice tests so you'll be able to get started on preparing for the test. The practice tests are going to be broken down into two sections. The first section is going to be short practice tests for when you don't have a lot of time and want a quick test or need a short test to help you see what areas you need to study further. Then, in the second section, we'll provide a full-length test that you can time yourself and check your answers just like the real thing to help you see when you're ready to take the real exam.

# Short Practice Tests

## Practice Test #1

1. Donald is managing a new project for a radio-operated model plane. The budget for the project is set at $200,000 and must be finished within six months of the start date. What is the name of the document that authorizes this project and gives Donald the authority to apply organizational resources to the project?

A. Project Charter

B. Scope Statement

C. Project Management Plan

D. Organization Process Assets

2. Which of the following statements is true, considering the levels of both cost and risk vary

throughout the project life cycle?

A. At the initiating stage, costs are high, and risk is low.

B. At the initiating stage, both costs and risks are high.

C. At the initiating stage, costs and risk are low.

D. At the initiating stage, both costs and risks are low.

3. Phase-end meetings are used in a phased project to sign-off on the deliverables associated with a specific phase. These phase end points often provide a good chance to evaluate the progress and performance of the phase. Which of the following terms is synonymous with phase end?

A. Phase exits

B. Kill points

C. Milestones

D. All of the above

4. A company manufacturing office furniture initiates a project to computerize and automate some of its manufacturing processes. Manufacturing personnel aren't happy with this idea and are afraid they will lose their jobs to automation. What is the first step a project manager should take?

A. Create a probability and impact matrix.

B. Include manufacturing personnel as project stakeholders.

C. Meet with manufacturing employees and tell them their jobs are safe.

D. Meet with the sponsor to get their advice.

5. A critical aspect of managing a project is stakeholder management. The project manager needs to come up with a strategy in order to manage stakeholder expectations. What is one technique that can be used to develop this strategy?

A. Issue log.

B. Stakeholder analysis.

C. Stakeholder register.

D. Stakeholder management plan.

6. The project manager is tasked with sorting, reviewing and analyzing a large number of ideas on requirements provided by various stakeholders. To accomplish this, which of the following tools can be utilized?

A. Affinity Diagram.

B. Mind Mapping.

C. Pareto Chart.

D. Brainstorming.

7. In the Develop Project Management Plan process, which of the following are inputs?

A. Project Charter

B. Enterprise Environmental Factors

C. Expert Judgment

D. Both a and b

8. The EV or Earned Value for an operating system design project is calculated at $300,000. The AC or Actual

Cost is $280,000. The BAC or Budget at Completion is estimated at $500,000. From a budgetary point of view, the project is progressing well since the CPI value is greater than one. What is the EAC or Estimate at Completion if the future work of the project is performed at the budgeted rate?

EV = 300,000
AC = 280,000
BAC = 500k
CPI = 1·07

A. $580,000

B. $480,000

C. $780,000

D. $500,000

9. The EV for an optic radar design project is calculated at $100,000, and the AC is $80,000. The BAC is estimated at $200,000. What is the current CPI or Cost Performance Index for this project?

A. 0.80

B. 0.50

C. 2.50

D. 1.25

$$CP = \frac{EV}{AC} = \frac{100\,000}{80,000}$$

10. Leads and lags on a project schedule network diagram are used to define the relationships between activities. The leads and lags indicate either acceleration or delay of the successor activity. If a team member on the project indicates FF+3 on the network diagram, what does this notation indicate?

A. Activities with a Finish-to-Finish relationship and three days of lag time.

B. The activity has three days of final float.

C. Activity with a Finish-to-Finish relationship and three days of lead time.

D. None of the above.

11. With the Manage Stakeholder Engagement process, which of the following are inputs?

A. Issue log and performance reports.

B. Change log and enterprise environmental factors.

C. Change log and risk register.

D. Stakeholder management plan and change log.

12. Various methods are used to disseminate information in project communications. Communication can take the form of formal, informal, verbal and nonverbal methods. Which of the following defines direct communication with your peers?

A. Formal

B. Horizontal

C. External

D. Vertical

13. Earned value analysis is a method for measuring the project performance. Project managers use this analysis to plan for risks based on the actual cost, schedule and progress of the work. If a project during the executing phase has negative values for the cost variance and the schedule variance, which of the following most accurately represents the project's status?

A. The project is ahead of schedule and under budget.

B. The project is behind schedule and under budget.

C. The project is over budget and behind schedule.

D. The project is ahead of schedule and over budget.

14. Clark is managing a project that builds non-nuclear components for nuclear weapons. The team consists of scientists, engineers, designers and technical experts with extensive backgrounds in their respective fields. Clark initiates a kickoff meeting with all team members in an effort to create a degree of trust among the team members. At the meeting, Clark wants to clarify the objective of the project and learn about the interests and levels of influence of each team member. Clark also needs to assign the roles and responsibilities for the team members. Based on this scenario, which of the following stages is the team in?

A. Storming

B. Performing

C. Norming

D. Forming

15. During the project execution, the planned value, earned value and the actual cost all have identical values. Based on this scenario, which of the following best describes the status of the project?

A. The project is over budget and behind schedule.

B. The cost variance and the schedule variance values are positive.

C. The project is on schedule and on budget.

D. The cost performance index and the schedule performance index values are zero.

16. One standard deviation is equal to 0.02. Using this, what is the upper control limit in a control chart if the upper control limit is set at +2 Sigma?

A. 0.4

B. 0.04

C. 0.02

D. 0.01

17. Rouge Systems in three weeks into a 5-week project to consolidate all of their data servers to a central location in a new data center. The amount of money spent to date is about $80,000. The planned value for the move at the three-week mark is $50,000. What is the status of the project?

A. On time

B. Behind schedule

C. Ahead of schedule

D. Over budget

18. Jacob finished the requirements documentation, including the deliverable acceptance criteria, to determine the success of the project in terms of the deliverable produced. The criteria include a series of tasks. Jacob and the customer need to perform a series of tasks in order to complete the acceptance and sign-off of final deliverables. Which project processes use this criterion to provide formal acceptance of the deliverables?

A. Control Scope

B. Close Project

C. Control Quality

D. Validated Scope

19. Which of the following processes are used to describe the collection, measurement, and distribution of performance information and measure the health of the project to identify project areas that require corrective or preventive actions?

A. Direct and manage project execution.

B. Monitor and control project work.

C. Integrated change control.

D. None of the above.

20. Wanda is examining the data on her control chart. The chart shows four consecutive points about +3 Sigma and three subsequent points below -3 Sigma. The lower and upper control limits are set at +-3 Sigma. What is the status of the process?

A. The process is out of control.

B. The process doesn't need improvement.

C. The process is under control.

D. Status cannot be determined with only seven data

points.

21. A municipal organization has a project for a crime prevention software program. A steering committee is responsible for approving all deliverables before being transferred to operations. The steering committee is composed of directors from three municipal agencies. If the steering committee approves the transfer of deliverables with a 2-1 vote, which statement below is correct?

A. The project is in the close scope phase.

B. The project is in the close project phase.

C. The project is in the control procurements phase.

D. The project is in the validate scope phase.

22. Debra just took over an IT project. The project was

terminated six months ago because of a shortage of funds and resources. Debra wants to determine why there was a shortage of funds as well as the situation with the incomplete deliverables. Which of the following documents should Debra examine in order to get the facts of the project?

A. Project management plan

B. Historical database

C. Project closure documents

D. Lessons learned documents

23. A project manager needs to measure prior information from the previous phase closures in order to ensure that all project deliverables are complete during project closure. Which of the following documents should the project manager use and review to measure project scope and ensure completion of deliverables before a project is considered closed?

A. Scope management plan

B. Project charter

C. Project management plan

D. Work breakdown structure

24. Adrian is managing a new project and has spent the last several days meeting with key project resources to review his procurements. What project process is involved if Adrian tells his team to close all inventory and contract management records to update the final procurement results?

A. Close project

B. Control costs

C. Control procurements

D. Conduct procurements

25. Which of the following is involved in the administrative closure of a project?

A. Activities necessary to audit project failure.

B. Activities necessary to transfer the end product.

C. Activities necessary to satisfy the exit criteria for the project.

D. All of the above.

# Answer Key #1

1. A - The project charter records the description of the project and its requirements while also authorizing the use of organizational resources to produce the objective of the project. The scope statement and project management

plan contain an elaborate version of these requirements. The organization's process assets are a set of policies, procedures and guidelines meant to ensure the success of the project.

2. C - Costs are typically low at the initiating stage of the project. Uncertainty is high at the initiating stage, meaning the risks associated are also high. As the project continues, resources are expanded, causing costs to rise. As the project nears completion, the uncertainty and associated risk is lowered.

3. D - All terms are synonymous with phase end points.

4. B - Some stakeholders benefit from a project, but others can be negatively impacted. The project manager is responsible for identifying both of these groups of stakeholders. Failing to recognize the negatively impacted stakeholders can have an impact on project objectives. Meeting with a sponsor may not resolve the issue, especially if you haven't heard the concerns of the negative stakeholders yet. Therefore, your first step is to include the manufacturing personnel as project stakeholders. A logical next step may be to create a probability and impact matrix, but without analysis of the

impact and its probability, you shouldn't assure employees that their jobs aren't in jeopardy.

5. B - Stakeholder analysis is the process of defining the stakeholder management strategy and includes specific information like the identities of those stakeholders who can have a major impact on the project and their level of participation. The issue log evolves while managing stakeholder expectations and can result in change orders to incorporate corrective or preventive actions. The stakeholder register is used to identify the project stakeholders. The stakeholder management plan identifies the strategies needed to effectively engage stakeholders.

6. A - Affinity diagrams are used to sort and group ideas for additional review and analysis. Mind mapping groups ideas based on similarities and differences. A Pareto chart is used to identify the 80/20 relationships of problems in the quality area. Brainstorming is a requirement-gathering technique primarily used in the idea generation stage rather than review and analysis.

7. D - Both the project charter and the enterprise environmental factors are inputs to the Develop Project

Management Process. While this process utilizes expert judgment, it is considered a tool and technique rather than an input.

8. B - The EAC or Estimate at Completion is the total cost of the project at completion. There are two ways to calculate EAC. It can be calculated at the budgeted rate or figured using the present CPI. The EAC at the budgeted rate is based on performance to date and represented by the actual accrued costs. The formula is the following: EAC = AC + BAC - EV

9. D - CPI is calculated by the following equation: CPI = EV/AC.

10. A - There are four types of relationships when sequencing activities: finish-to-finish, start-to-finish, finish-to-start, and start-to-start. FF indicated finish-to-finish. Leads are shown by a negative sign, and lags are indicated with a positive sign. Log +ve Lead -ve

11. D - All inputs to the manage stakeholder engagement process include the stakeholder management plan, communications management plan, change log and organizational process assets.

12. B - Formal communication includes reports, memos and briefings. Communication that goes outside the team or stakeholders is external communication.

13. C - Cost variance equals earned value minus actual costs (EV-AC). If the value is negative, it means the project is over budget. Schedule variance equals earned value minus planned value (EV-PV). If the value is negative, it means the project is behind schedule.

14. D - Team development goes through stages: Forming, Storming, Norming, Performing and Adjourning. Getting to know team members and preparing to assign roles and responsibilities is in the forming stage.

15. C - If the planned value, earned value and actual cost values are identical, then the cost variance and schedule variance values are zero. These values indicate the project is on schedule and on budget.

16. B - One Sigma in the control limit indicates one standard deviation. This means the upper control limit = +2 Sigma or +2 standard deviation.

17. B - EV is a measure of work performed in terms of

the budget authorized for the work. PV is the authorized budget assigned to schedule work to be accomplished for an activity at a given point in time or phase. If the EV is less than the PV, this is a scheduling issue. Since PV denotes how much work should be completed and EV denotes the actual work that is complete, there is less completed work than planned, meaning the project is behind schedule.

18. D - Validated deliverables are compared against the criteria for acceptance and requirements. This is required to formally sign-off the completed deliverables. The requirements documentation is an input to the validated scope process, and the deliverable acceptance criteria created in the planning phase are used in the validated scope process of the monitoring and controlling phase.

19. B - The monitor and control project work process measures the progress of the project. Monitoring activities include measuring, collecting, and distributing performance information and controlling activities, including determining corrective or preventive actions.

20. A - Seven consecutive points above or below the upper and lower control limits indicate a process that is

out of control.

21. B - A project is considered closed when all deliverables are transferred and lessons learned documentation, project files and historical databases are updated.

22. C - Project closure documents contain information related to the deliverables and other closing documents. If the project is terminated, the documents would indicate why the project was terminated early.

23. C - Project scope is measured against the project management plan. The project management plan should be reviewed by the project manager to verify the project scope has been achieved and to ensure deliverables are complete.

24. C - During the control procurements process, all contract results are updated and all procurement documents are closed.

25. D - The activities required to perform an administrative closure of a project include activities necessary to satisfy the exit criteria of a project, the activities necessary to transfer the project's result and the

activities necessary to audit project success or failure.

# Practice Test #2

1. A project manager is assigned the task of managing a software development project that involves implementing new and emerging technology. The team is unsure about the complexity and potential issues that might come up during the project. In order to manage the technical uncertainties of this project, the project manager should use which of the following most appropriate approaches?

A. Conduct research, engage subject matter experts, and perform a pilot implementation of the new technology to gain experience and mitigate risks.

B. Conduct research and engage subject matter experts, but avoid discussing or identifying potential risks associated with the new technology.

C. Ignore the uncertainties and proceed with the project as planned without any adjustments.

D. Outsource the entire project to a third-party vendor with experience in the new technology.

2. A project manager is assigned a new product launch that has recently gained significant media attention. The social and market influences are causing doubts among the stakeholders about the project's success. What should the project manager do?

A. Engage with stakeholders proactively, address their concerns, and develop a plan to mitigate the impact of media attention on the success of the project.

B. Postpone the project until the media attention fades and the stakeholders regain their confidence.

C. Engage with the stakeholders proactively, address their concerns, and adapt communication strategies to maintain their confidence in the project.

D. Ignore the media attention and continue with the project as planned without addressing stakeholder concerns.

3. A project manager is working with a team to develop a new product in a highly competitive market. The team identified several uncertainties linked to the project, which could have various outcomes. The project manager needs to determine the best approach to deal with these uncertainties. Which of the following is the best approach?

A. Focus on the threats and ignore any opportunities that arise to avoid distracting the team from the primary objectives.

B. Gather information through research, engage experts, or perform a market analysis to reduce uncertainty and make informed decisions.

C. Make decisions based on the intuition of the team and past experiences without gathering additional information.

D. Postpone the project until the uncertainties are gone, and the project can proceed without risks.

4. Using a probabilistic estimate derived from a computer simulation, a project manager estimates the cost of a project. The point estimate is $100,000 with a range of +$10,000/-$5,000. The project manager is 90% confident that the actual cost will stay within this range. The probability distribution is a triangular distribution. What is the standard distribution in this situation?

SD

A. $2,500

B. $3,000

C. $3,500

D. $4,000

5. Using both absolute and relative estimating

techniques, a project manager estimates the duration of two tasks: A and B. Task A is estimated to take 120 hours of work, and one person working full time can complete the task in 15 days, assuming 8 hours of productivity per workday. Take B is estimated to take 50% more effort than Task A. How many hours of work are estimated for Task B using absolute estimating?

A= 120hr (8hr x 15d)

A. 150

B. 180

C. 200

D. 220

6. The project manager notices that the cost incurred in the first phase of the execution of a software development project is significantly higher than what was allocated in the cost baseline. The project accounted for both contingency and management reserves. What action should the project manager take?

A. Request additional funds from the sponsor to cover the increased costs.

B. Utilize the contingency reserve to cover the additional costs.

C. Reassess the project budget and reschedule the work to align with the current funding limitations.

D. Utilize the management reserve to cover the additional costs.

7. A project has a CPI of 0.94 and a schedule performance index or SPI of 1.05. Using this information, what is the current status of the project?

A. Behind schedule and over budget.

B. Behind schedule and within budget.

C. Ahead of schedule and within budget.

D. Ahead of schedule and over budget.

8. A project manager wants to track the progress of an agile project using visual controls. The team has completed a significant amount of work and the project manager wants to measure the productivity rate of the team with a visual chart. What is the next step the project manager should take?

A. Use a task board to track the project's progress.

B. Use a burnup chart to track the amount of work done compared to the expected work that should be done.

C. Use a burndown chart to track the number of story points remaining or the amount of risk exposure that has been reduced.

D. Use an impediment list to show a description of the impediment to getting work done, the severity, and the actions being taken to resolve the impediment.

9. A construction project manager has a contract with a supplier to deliver materials. During the project execution, the project manager realizes the need to change the quantity of materials to be delivered, which will have an impact on the project's budget and schedule. What should the project manager do next?

A. Assume that there is no defined process for contract changes.

B. Make changes to the contract as needed.

C. Inform the supplier of the changes and negotiate a new contract.

D. Submit a change request to the change control board or CCB and follow the change control process.

10. A project manager is leading a team on a construction project. The budget is $500,000 with a

planned duration of six months. At the end of three months, the team reports spending $350,000 and only 30% completion. Based on this information, what can be concluded about the performance?

EV = $150
PV = $250
AC = 350

A. The project is on track since 50% of the time has passed, and 30% of the work has been completed, but more information is needed to determine budget status.

B. The project is ahead of schedule and over budget since only 30% of the work has been completed at a halfway point, and $350,000 of the budget has already been spent.

C. The project is on budget since the time has only been spent 70% so far, but more information is needed to determine the schedule status.

D. The project is behind schedule and over budget, since only 30% of the work has been completed at the halfway point and $350,000 of the budget is already spent.

11. For a few months, a project manager has been leading a team on a software development project. The project is behind schedule, and the team is facing many issues, including a lack of motivation and conflicts. The project manager is concerned about the impact these issues have on the project and the morale of the team. What could the project manager have done to prevent this situation?

A. Implement a mood chart to track the team's moods and identify potential issues early.

B. Ignore the issues and focus on completing the project as fast as possible.

C. Offer incentives and rewards to high-performing team members to increase motivation and reduce conflicts.

D. Hire new team members to replace those who are not motivated or causing conflicts.

12. A project manager is overseeing a software development project with a tight deadline that the team is working diligently to meet. However, the project manager realizes the team is falling behind schedule and potentially won't meet the deadline. The project manager panics and starts to micromanage the team, which only slows down the work further. What could the project manager have done to prevent this situation?

A. From the start, set realistic timelines and ensured the team had the appropriate resources to meet them.

B. Push the team harder to meet the deadline, even if it affects quality.

C. Negotiate with the sponsor to extend the end date of the project.

D. Continue to micromanage and provide constant supervision to ensure the team stays on track.

13. A project manager is assigned a software

development project. The team is having a hard time keeping track of the tasks and their progress. The project manager wants to find a tool to track and manage the tasks more effectively. What next step should the project manager take?

A. Use a spreadsheet to track the tasks and their progress.

B. Implement a project management software to manage tasks and progress.

C. Assign a team member to track tasks and report in daily meetings.

D. Ignore the challenges and continue to work on the project as normal.

14. A project manager notices that the KPIs or key performance indicators used to track project processes are not relevant anymore due to a change in requirements. What should the project manager do?

A. Continue to report the KPIs as is, and don't make any changes.

B. Create new KPIs and communicate them to the stakeholders.

C. Meet with the stakeholders to discuss and agree on new KPIs.

D. Stop reporting KPIs altogether.

15. A project manager wants to use EVM performance indices to provide feedback and calculate KPIs segmented by the project team. What is the next step for the project manager?

A. Work with the project team to collect and compile data needed to calculate the KPIs.

B. Forward the issue to the program manager and

request help in calculating the KPIs.

C. Work with the finance team to calculate the KPIs based on EVM performance indices.

D. Ask the project sponsor for guidance in calculating KPIs.

16. A software team is deciding when to run regression tests to maintain product quality without sacrificing build performance. Which of the following is a useful guide for the team to use?

A. Ignore regression tests for agile teams.

B. Decide when to run regression tests and which ones to use.

C. Run regression tests only at the start of a project.

D. Focus only on new tests and don't revisit old ones.

17. A team working on a software development project has been experiencing scope creep and customer dissatisfaction. As the project manager, you have identified that ineffective requirements management is the main cause. What next step would you take to address this issue?

A. Implement a strict change control process to prevent further changes to the project scope.

B. Increase the frequency of project status meetings to keep stakeholders informed about the progress.

C. Focus the team solely on the initial requirements to avoid further scope creep.

D. Assign a dedicated individual to manage requirements using tools such as traceability matrices or backlogs.

18. A new team is attempting to adopt agile and finds themselves having difficulty demonstrating or releasing

their working product frequently. What is a possible implication of this situation?

A. The team is likely efficient in adopting agile techniques.

B. There is no need for external coaching.

C. The team may require additional coaching to enable frequent delivery.

D. The team should switch back to traditional project management.

19. An organization wants to evolve its methods while tracking its progress. What tool can help them to visualize the new approaches being tried, those in use and those waiting for introduction?

A. A Gantt chart that shows all change projects.

B. A Kanban board that indicates the status of each approach.

C. A financial spreadsheet that outlines the cost of each change.

D. A list of changes that is sent by email to all teams.

20. A project manager is aware that two team members are going to be on vacation during the next iteration. In terms of story commitment for that iteration, what should the project manager expect?

A. The team will commit to more stories to compensate for the absence.

B. The team will commit to the same number of stores as the previous iteration.

C. The team's commitment will be unrelated to the members' absences.

D. The team will commit to fewer stories because of the reduced capacity.

21. A project team is looking to use their new software to understand the flow of a user's action. What technique can be used to gain this understanding?

A. Only focus on end-to-end system-level testing.

B. Prioritizing documentation over experimentation.

C. Utilizing spikes.

D. Avoiding any type of testing.

22. A team on day three of iteration, reviews a burndown chart and sees they aren't on track with their plan. What should the team take from this information?

A. The team has overdelivered and can relax.

B. The team is at risk for that delivery.

C. The burndown chart isn't helpful.

D. The team's original estimation was perfect.

23. A software team is deciding when to run regression tests to maintain product quality without affecting build performance. What would be a useful guideline for the team?

A. Ignore regression tests for agile teams.

B. Decide when to run regression tests and which ones to use.

C. Run regression tests at the start of the project only.

D. Focus only on new tests and never revisit old ones.

24. A team is facing challenges with consistently delivering value. What should the team emphasize in order to enhance their speed of delivery without compromising quality?

A. Avoid all testing.

B. Prioritize technical practices from extreme programming.

C. Rely entirely on manual testing methods.

D. Focus only on end-user feedback.

25. The initial prototype of a new product during a product development project receives negative feedback from potential users. The project manager recognizes a need for a rapid and effective response to this feedback. What immediate action should the project manager take to demonstrate resilience?

A. Continue with product development, assuming users will adapt to the product in time.

B. Disband the current project team and form a new one to get fresh perspectives.

C. Initiate a thorough review of the feedback and quickly adapt the product design to better meet the needs of users.

D. Escalate the issue to higher management for a decision on whether or not to halt the project.

# Answer Key #2

1. A - Doing things in this order allows a project manager and their team to gain experience and mitigate the risks associated with the technology. This approach allows the team to understand the potential challenges and develop solutions to address any issues that may come up. This allows the project manager to effectively manage the technical uncertainties and minimize potential negative impacts on the project.

2. C - Using this approach ensures stakeholders are informed and involved, which helps to build support and trust for the project. The project manager can mitigate the potential negative impact of social and market influences on the success of the project by addressing stakeholder concerns and adapting communication strategies.

3. B - Using this approach helps to address both opportunities and threats. It allows the project manager to better manage the risks of the project and make well-informed decisions that are in line with the project objectives.

4. B - To calculate the standard deviation of the probability distribution, you use the following formula: Standard deviation = (maximum-minimum) / (2 x square root of 6). The maximum and minimum are the upper and lower limits of the triangular distribution.

5. B - Task A is estimated to take 120 hours of work. Task B is estimated to take 50% more effort than Task A. This means it will take 1.5 times the effort of Task A. Absolute estimating is used to provide specific information and use actual numbers.

6. C - The scenario suggests that contingency reserves for uncertainty and management reserves for unexpected in-scope activities. Increased costs in the first phase indicate a potential deviation from the cost baseline. Reassessing the project budget and rescheduling the work is the best option since it ensures alignment with the existing funding limitations. Utilizing contingency or management reserves at this stage may not be appropriate since they are typically used for unforeseen events or in-scope changes, not initial budget overruns. Requesting additional funds should only be considered after a thorough reassessment and only when absolutely necessary.

7. D - The CPI is a measure of the cost efficiency of a project. A CPI greater than one indicates that the project is under budget, while a CPI less than one indicates that the project is over budget. The SPI is a measure of the schedule efficiency of a project. An SPI greater than one indicates that the project is ahead of schedule, while an SPI less than one indicates that the project is behind schedule.

8. B - Burnup charts can track the amount of work completed compared to the expected work that needs to be

done. Project managers can use these to understand the overall progress of the project and can provide insight into whether or not a project is on track. On the other hand, burndown charts show the number of story points remaining or the amount of risk exposure that has been reduced to help project managers monitor the overall health of a project and ensure it is moving in the right direction.

9. D - For projects with a contractual element, any changes to the contract need to follow a defined process. The change control process ensures any changes to the project, including changes to the contract, are properly reviewed and approved by appropriate parties before implementation.

10. D - A project manager can calculate the SPI and the CPI to help assess project performance. The SPI indicates how efficiently the scheduled work is being performed. The CPI indicates how efficiently the work is being performed in relation to the budgeted cost of the work.

11. A - Using a mood chart, allows the project manager to track the morale of the team and address issues before them become a bigger issue. It can also identify issues

between team members or lack of motivation. The project manager can address issues early on by taking corrective action and preventing them from having an impact on the project.

12. A - A key reason to use measures is to assess if project deliverables are on track to deliver planned benefits.

13. B - Task boards can provide a visual representation of the planned work. This allows everyone to see the status of the tasks. It will show work that is ready to be started, work in progress, and work that is completed. This allows a project manager to effectively track and manage the tasks.

14. C - Since project requirements have changed, it is essential that the project manager meet with the stakeholders to discuss and agree on new KPIs that are relevant to the new requirements. Any other option is going to provide an inaccurate representation of the progress of the project. The project manager shouldn't stop using KPIs because they are crucial to the tracking process and help identify potential issues.

15. A - The project manager is responsible for

managing the team and tracking project performance. By working with the project team, the project manager can gather and compile the data needed to calculate KPIs using EVM performance indices.

16. B - Agile teams benefit from strategically deciding when to run regression tests and choosing the specific tests to run. This helps to maintain product quality while ensuring good build performance. These tests help to ensure that previously developed functionalities still work as expected after adding new changes.

17. D - Assigning a dedicated individual to manage requirements is key for addressing issues related to scope creep and customer dissatisfaction. Various methods, such as backlogs and traceability matrices, can be used to balance requirement flexibility and stability, ensuring new and changing requirements are managed effectively and agreed upon by relevant stakeholders.

18. C - Being unable to frequently demonstrate or release a working product can be a sign that the team isn't adopting agile techniques as they should. External coaching can help the team align with agile principles.

19. B - A Kanban board provides a visual

representation of the flow and status of tasks. It can categorize new approaches as "complete," those being tried as "in progress," and those pending as "to do."

20. D - When team members are unavailable, the team has reduced capacity. This means the team won't be able to finish the same amount of work as they did in the previous time period.

21. C - Spikes provide a method for teams to conduct timeboxed research or experiments. These are especially useful when the team needs to understand some critical technical or functional element, such as the flow of a user's action.

22. B - From the information provided, the team can see they are not following the planned dotted line. This indicates that they are at risk for that delivery.

23. B - Agile teams benefit from strategically deciding when to run regression tests and choosing the correct tests to run. This can help maintain product quality while also ensuring good build performance. This also helps the team to ensure that previously developed functionalities still work after new changes.

x24. B - Technical practices from extreme programming, such as continuous integration, testing at all levels, and test-driven development, can help teams deliver at maximum speed without affecting quality. These practices help to ensure the product is robust, client expectations are met, and things can be delivered rapidly.

25. C - The correct and immediate thing to do is to review the feedback and use it to change the product accordingly to make it easier for the user.

# Practice Test #3

1. The head of engineering and a manager are discussing changes to a major work package. Following the meeting, the manager contacts you and tells you to complete the paperwork needed to make the change. What is this an example of?

A. Management attention to scope management.

B. Management planning.

C. A project expediter position.

D. A change control system.

2. During a team meeting, a team member asks about measurements that are going to be used on the project to judge performance. They feel that some of the measures related to the activities assigned to them aren't valid measurements. What part of the project management process is this project in?

A. Initiating

B. Executing

C. Monitoring and Controlling

D. Closing

3. Your company won a new project that starts in three months and is valued at two million. You are a project manager working on an existing project. What's the first

thing you should do when you learn about a new project?

A. Ask management how resources will be used for the new project.

B. Resource level your project.

C. Crash your project.

D. Ask management how the new project will affect your existing project.

4. You are a new project manager who hasn't managed a project before. During planning, what should you rely on in order to improve your chance of success?

A. Intuition and training.

B. Stakeholder analysis.

C. Historical information.

D. Configuration management.

5. A team member comes to the project manager during project execution because they aren't sure what work they need to accomplish on the project. Which document would contain detailed descriptions of work packages?

A. WBS Dictionary

B. Activity List

C. Project Scope Statement

D. Scope Management Plan

6. The project manager meets with some stakeholders and is asked to add work to the project scope. The project manager has access to correspondence from before the project charter was signed and remembers that the project sponsor specifically denied funding for the scope

that the stakeholders are asking for. What is the best thing for the project manager to do?

A. Tell the sponsor about the stakeholder's request.

B. Evaluate the impact of adding scope.

C. Tell the stakeholders the scope can't be added.

D. Add the work if the time is available in the project.

7. The project management plan results in a project schedule that is too long. What is the best thing to do if the project network diagram can't change but you have extra personnel resources?

A. Fast-track the project.

B. Level the resources.

C. Crash the project.

D. Monte Carlo analysis.

8. An activity has an ES or early start on day three, an LS or late start on day thirteen, an EF or early finish on day nine, and an LF or late finish on day nineteen. Which of the following is true for the activity?

A. Is on the critical path.

B. Has a lag.

C. Is progressing well.

D. Is not on the critical path.

9. Early in a project, you are having a discussion with the sponsor about what estimating techniques to use. You want a type of expert judgment, but the sponsor wants analogous estimating. What is the best course of action?

A. Agree to the analogous estimating since it is a form of expert judgment.

B. Suggest life cycle costing.

C. Determine why the sponsor wants an accurate estimate.

D. Try to convince the sponsor for expert judgment because it is often more accurate.

10. Susan is working as a Scrum Master in a Scrum Team. The team consists of five developers. Ronald is one of the developers. Susan notices that Ronald is applying a different approach to complete Sprint tasks faster. What is the best thing for Susan to do?

A. Call immediately for a team meeting and tell them that Ronald has a new approach to completing tasks faster.

B. Ask Ronald to stop his task and prepare a detailed

guide on how to apply his approach, then distribute it to the team.

C. During the retrospective, ask Ronald to share his approach with the team and ask if it is applicable to every developer.

D. Ask Ronald in the next daily standup meeting why he didn't share his approach with the team.

11. You are a program-level manager and have several project activities in the works. During the executing process group, you are concerned about the accuracy of progress reports from the projects. What can help you support your opinion?

A. Quality audits.

B. Risk quantification reports.

C. Regression analysis.

D. Monte Carlo analysis.

12. You are a project manager for a large cloud project. A member of the quality department contacts you about starting a quality audit of the project. The team objects to the audit because they are already under pressure to complete the project as fast as possible. You need to explain the purpose of the quality audit to the team.

A. Part of an ISO 9000 investigation.

B. To see if the customer is following its quality process.

C. To identify inefficient and ineffective policies.

D. To check the accuracy of costs submitted by the team.

13. The project manager asks each team member

during a project meeting to describe the work they are doing. The project manager then assigns new activities to each team member. The length of the meetings has increased because of the number of activities to assign. This can happen for all except which of the following?

A. Lack of a WBS.

B. Lack of a responsibility assignment matrix.

C. Lack of resource leveling.

D. Lack of team involvement in project planning.

14. Your friend Andy works as a software developer at an E-commerce company. Andy is talking with you about the project and mentions that the project management approach relies on three practices: 1) Visualize what you do today, 2) Limit the amount of work in progress, and 3) Enhance flow. Andy's project is using which of the following agile methodologies?

A. Kanban

B. Lean

C. Scrum

D. Extreme Programming

15. You are working as a project manager for a company that produces healthcare products. You are constantly monitoring the business environment for changes that can impact your project. For environmental scanning, you are using pestel analysis. Which of the following is not a pestel category?

A. You are in the US healthcare market and the FDA launched a new regulation for healthcare products.

B. There is political tension with a country, and they have banned the use of your company's products in their country.

C. A competitor to your company has launched a new technological product that can change the market.

D. A member of your project team has just resigned and you hear rumors they will start working for the competition.

16. A project manager is quantifying risk for a project and needs an expert opinion on the process. Related experts are spread over different geographical locations. How should the project manager proceed?

A. Use a Monte Carlo analysis online.

B. Apply the critical path method.

C. Determine options for recommended corrective action.

D. Apply the Delphi Technique.

17. After risk management activities, 236 risks were identified as caused by 13 root causes. Through risk management activities, you could eliminate 234 risks. For the final two risks, the team cannot find a way to mitigate or insure the risks. These two risks also can't be outsourced or removed from the project scope. What is the appropriate solution?

A. Accept the risk

B. Mitigate the risk

C. Avoid the risk

D. Transfer the risk

18. The project team is arguing about submitted proposals from prospective sellers. One team member wants a certain seller, while another team member wants the project awarded to another seller. To remind the team

in making a selection, what is the best thing the project manager can do?

A. Procurement documents

B. Procurement audits

C. Evaluation criteria

D. Procurement management plan

19. A project manager is creating an RFP or Request for Proposal. What stage of the procurement process are they in?

A. Conduct procurements

B. Plan procurements

C. Control procurements

D. Close procurements

20. Which of the following is the appropriate model for grouping project stakeholders based on authority and involvement in the project?

A. Power/Interest Grid

B. Power/Influence Grid

C. Influence/Impact Grid

D. Salience Model

21. Katherine works at a business consulting company. One of the clients asked the company to prepare a project management approach that fits their company. Katherine works on this project and finds that agile methods are a good fit for the company. Of the following, what doesn't fit into the values of the agile manifesto?

A. Individuals and interactions.

B. Comprehensive documentation.

C. Customer collaboration.

D. Responding to change over following a plan.

22. All of the following statements except one are correct in the context of a desirable model of communication between sender and receiver.

A. Noise should be kept to a minimum level.

B. The receiver must reply to the message after decoding.

C. The receiver should acknowledge first and then agree with the message from the sender.

D. The receiver should send a feedback message to the

sender.

23. Jake is the project manager on a complicated project. Upon creating a work breakdown structure for the project, Jake realized it was too complicated to have a work breakdown structure on a single sheet. You recommend Jake to use a work breakdown structure numbering system in order to do which of the following?

A. Determine the complexity of the project.

B. Help in automating the WBS using appropriate software.

C. Provide a hierarchical structure for each WBS element.

D. Present risks of the project.

24. You can use all of the following except one when

trying to establish a cost performance baseline for a project in the Determine Budget Process.

A. Cost aggregation.

B. Bottom-up estimating.

C. Expert judgment.

D. Historical relationships.

25. Which of the following techniques includes measuring, examining, and validating whether deliverables and work meet requirements and product acceptance criteria?

A. Workshops

B. Surveys

C. Expert judgment

D. Inspection

26. You are a project manager for a bicycle manufacturing company. The rubber used for the brake mechanism couldn't reach the facility due to flood-affected transportation routes. You thought this risk could happen since it is an issue that comes up each year in the same season. Per the risk response plan, you start to use the rubber from the previous shipment. However, this presents a new risk since old rubber has a higher breaking risk during the implementation of the braking system. What can this new risk also be called?

A. Secondary Risk

B. Residual Risk

C. Contingency Plan

D. Unmanageable Risks

27. Tim works as a project manager at a nationwide logistics company. Tim is responsible for managing a project that will optimize company vehicle delivery routes to reduce the cost of fuel. One of the project team members emailed Tim that they didn't understand the tasks clearly. What should Tim do next?

A. Reply via email to have them read the project scope document again.

B. Call the team members' functional manager and confirm that they are qualified to work on the project.

C. Arrange a meeting with the team member and try to understand what isn't clear.

D. Raise the issue at the next team meeting and ask the team to clarify things for the team member who is unclear.

28. As a project manager, you are expected to manage stakeholders' expectations. A project manager should

apply all of the following interpersonal skills except which one?

A. Building trust

B. Resolving conflict

C. Risk-taking

D. Active listening

29. Several changes in your project had an impact on your cost and schedule estimates. The original estimating assumptions have been invalidated. Based on the following parameters, what is the EAC or Estimate at Completion for the project?

BAC = $360,000

AC = $120,000

EV = $180,000

CPI = 1.2

ETC = $145,000

$$EAC = \frac{AC}{CPI} =$$

A. $300,000

B. $265,000

C. $325,000

D. $360,000

30. Sam works for a manufacturing company producing parts for automobiles. As a project management methodology, the company has adopted the Lean methodology. While Sam and his team are progressing through the project, a new requirement is requested. Another team member states that it is too late to accept new requirements. This other team member's behavior is against what?

A. Agile Values

B. Lean Manifesto

C. Agile Manifesto

D. Requirement-Driven Development

31. To develop a software program, your company enters into a joint venture with a service company. Both the buyer and seller should cooperatively prepare which of the following during the teaming agreement process?

A. Contract

B. Contract, Procurement statement of work

C. Request for proposal

D. Human resource plan

32. Your company has three possible projects to be executed:

Project A - Payback period = 6 years and NPV = $3,000,000

Project B - Payback period = 4 years and NPV = $2,000,000

Project C - Payback period = 2 years and NPV = $1,000,000

Based on the NPV or Net Present Value criterion, which project should your company choose?

A. Project A

B. Project B

C. Project C

D. None of them since they all have equal value.

33. Which technique is appropriate for gathering ideas related to a project and product requirements?

A. Brainstorming

B. Nominal Group Technique

C. Affinity Diagram

D. Multi-criteria Decision Analysis

34. Your colleague is a project manager who worked on an MP3 player development project. While discussing their experiences from the project, they mentioned that they delivered an extra feature without deviation from the plan even though the customer didn't require it and it wasn't in the scope of the project. The customer was

surprised and happy with the additional feature at the end of the project. Which of the following is correct?

A. Gold plating was done in the project.

B. Customer satisfaction increased with an additional feature they didn't expect.

C. Change request was delivered successfully.

D. Unnecessary risk was taken by adding a new feature to the product.

35. You document all possible risks that can have an impact on your project, along with appropriate risk responses in your risk management plan. What are all other remaining risks called?

A. Risk triggers.

B. Unmanageable risks.

C. Residual risks.

D. Accepted risks.

36. Working as the project manager for a company, you have the highest level of authority. You are working full-time on the project, and you are responsible for managing the entire project budget. What organization structure is the company?

A. Strong Matrix

B. Projectized

C. Functional

D. Balanced Matrix

37. You are the project manager for a software project team. The team consists of two analysts, four software developers and three test engineers. A new test engineer

will join the team in two weeks. What number of communication channels will there be after the new test engineer joins?

$$\frac{11 \times 10}{2.} \quad \frac{110}{2} = 55$$

A. 55

B. 50

C. 45

D. 36

38. Jackson is working at a fast-food company. The company initiated a project for process improvement after several complaints about the drive-thru process. Jackson completed the project and tracked the following benefits after completion; which of them is an intangible benefit?

A. After project completion, the number of drive-thru customers increased by 7%.

B. Drive-thru service complaints decreased by 88%.

C. In a survey, brand perception increased by 9% in relation to the drive-thru.

D. The average service cost per drive-thru customer decreased by 17% after the project was finished.

39. A seller's project is placed under contract and you are an employee of the seller. Since you worked on a project with the buyer before, you are aware of the evaluation criteria used by the company to select sellers. This could potentially be a conflict of interest. How should you proceed in this situation?

A. Do nothing and just work as before.

B. Take the appropriate person at the buyer's company into confidence and discuss the issue with them.

C. Disclose the evaluation criteria to the seller company to help their business grow.

D. Remove yourself from the project.

40. Which of the following steps comes last compared to others during the project planning phase?

A. Hold a kick-off meeting.

B. Gain formal approval of the plan.

C. Develop a budget.

D. Develop a schedule.

# Answer Key #3

1. C - The project manager is acting as the secretary of the project and is doing the paperwork. The project manager in the position of a project expediter doesn't have any authority or power. The project manager is only responsible for the paperwork.

2. B - Since the team member feels that some of the

measurements of their activities aren't valid, they must be working during the executing phase of the project, where deliverables are being produced, and project members are performing the majority of their assigned work.

3. D - Since this is another project that your company is going to execute, you need to know how it will impact your current project.

4. C - Before starting a new project, the first thing to explore is the historical information about similar projects in the organizational process assets library of the organization.

5. A - The WBS or Work Breakdown Structure Dictionary contains only nouns or a couple words regarding a deliverable or work. Detailed information on what needs to be done, responsible, prerequisites, successors, due date and more are included in the WBS Dictionary.

6. C - Once the scope of a project is finalized and the scope baseline is determined, it can only be changed if there is an approved change request. Without an approved change request, the existing scope baseline is

valid, and the project team needs to work on delivering the scope only. This means you need to inform the stakeholders that the new work can't be added.

7. C - If the schedule is too long, the aim is to make a shorter schedule. With extra personnel resources, you can put more resources into an activity to get it done in a shorter time. This is actually a description of crashing an activity or crashing the project.

8. D - If you consider the ES and LS values for the activity, you can determine the float or the slack of the activity's time by subtracting the ES 3 days from the LS, thirteen days. This gives 10 days of float for the activity. You can get the same result by subtracting the EF nine days from the LF nineteen days. Since the float of the activity is greater than zero, it's not on the critical path. Critical path activities have zero floats.

9. A - Analogous estimating is a form of expert judgment that you can accept.

10. C - The retrospective is an opportunity to inspect the team's performance and create a plan of improvement. The goal of this activity is to inspect and improve the process.

11. A - To check whether the standards of your organization are applied in projects under your responsibility, you can do a quality audit and determine whether or not there is a problem.

12. C - The best option is to explain the quality audit to the team as a way to identify inefficient and ineffective policies.

13. C - Lack of resource leveling can be the cause of a scheduling problem. Resource leveling is a technique used in the schedule management knowledge area, which helps with the uniform distribution of tasks and activities within a project.

14. A - Kanban has three basic practices. The first is to visualize what you do today. Seeing all items in the context of each other is informative. All work that is in progress, completed and in the queue is visualized on a board. The second is to limit the amount of work in progress. This helps to balance the flow-based approach so teams don't commit to too much work at once. Otherwise, too much work overburdens the team and causes quality to decrease. The third is to enhance flow. Once something is finished, the next highest priority from

the backlog is started.

15. D - Pestel stands for (Political, Economic, Social, Technological, Environmental, Legal). An environmental scan is the process of gathering, analyzing and interpreting data about external opportunities and threats.

16. D - The Delphi Technique asks the experts' opinions on a topic or a problem and collects their feedback anonymously. Then, the responses are sent back to the experts again, and their responses are collected again. The process is reiterated until a consensus is reached among all participants and experts. Since expert opinion is needed in this scenario and they are spread out over a geographical area, then this is the technique needed.

17. A - The project manager has already tried to eliminate, mitigate and transfer the risk. Therefore, the last step is to accept the risk. Continuous reserves should be allocated to accommodate risks to overcome the bad impacts of the risk.

18. C - The evaluation criteria are defined in the plan procurement management process. It defines in an objective, quantitative manner how potential sellers are

evaluated in the conduct procurements process. The sellers who receive the highest scores should be awarded the contract.

19. B - The procurement statement of work and procurement documents are prepared in the plan procurements management process. The RFP is a procurement document.

20. B - The authority of a stakeholder represents their power, and the involvement of a stakeholder represents their influence.

21. B - The Agile Manifesto has four values: 1) Individuals and interactions over processes and tools. 2) Working software. 3) Customer collaboration over contract negotiation. 4) Responding to change over following a plan.

22. C - As a part of the communication process, the sender transmits the message and is responsible for ensuring it is clear and complete. The sender is also responsible for confirming the communication is understood correctly. The responsibility of the receiver is to ensure the message is received in its entirety, understood correctly, and appropriately acknowledged or

responded to. The receiver doesn't have to agree with the message.

23. C - The WBS is finalized by assigning a work package to a control account and establishing a unique identifier from a code of accounts. These identifiers provide the structure for the hierarchical summation of costs, schedules and resource information.

24. B - Bottom-up estimating is used in the Estimate Costs Process. The other items on the list are a part of the Determine Budget Process.

25. D - Inspection is the only technique that includes all of the activities listed.

26. A - Secondary risks arise as a direct result of implementing a risk response.

27. C - Servant leadership is characterized by listening, empathy, and stewardship. Before taking further action, the project manager should understand what isn't clear or why the team member didn't understand the task.

28. C - The four main interpersonal skills a project manager can use to manage stakeholders' expectations

are 1) Building trust. 2) Resolving conflict. 3) Active listening. 4) Overcoming resistance to change.

29. B - The formula is EAC = AC + ETC

30. C - Lean methodology requires welcoming changing requirements, no matter where in development they happen. Agile processes harness change for the competitive advantage of the customer is one of the twelve principles in the Agile Manifesto.

31. B - Sometimes, the seller may already be working under a contract funded by the buyer or jointly by both parties. In this process, the effort of the buyer and seller is to collectively prepare a procurement statement of work that will meet the requirements of the project. The parties can then negotiate a final contract for the award.

32. A - Project A has the highest NPV. The time value of money is already taken into account when calculating the NPV. Therefore, since Project A has the highest NPV, it should be chosen.

33. A - Brainstorming is a technique that can be used to generate and collect multiple ideas related to a project and product requirements.

34. A - Gold plating is a term that refers to continuing to work on a project or task past the point where the extra effort is worth the value it adds.

35. C - Residual risks are expected to remain after planned responses have been taken, including those that have been deliberately accepted.

36. B - The project manager has the highest level of authority in a company with a projectized organizational structure.

37. A - The number of potential communication channels is determined by the formula n(n-1)/2. N represents the number of stakeholders. After the new test engineer joins, the team will consist of 11 members. The formula would apply: 11x(11-1)/2 = 11x10/2 = 55

38. C - Tangible benefits are monetary or financial benefits that a project brings to the company. Intangible benefits are non-monetary benefits that a project brings to the company. An increase in brand perception is an intangible benefit.

39. B - Since the evaluation criteria is the proprietary information of the buyer company, it is important to

discuss the matter directly with the appropriate person at that company.

40. A - In the planning phase, the following is the order of steps: Develop a schedule, develop a budget, gain formal approval of the plan, and hold a kick-off meeting. The kick-off meeting is the final step in the planning process.

---

# Practice Test #4

1. Due to other obligations, your sponsor will be leaving the project soon. They inform you the role will be filled by two new people. They assure you this shouldn't have an impact on communication complexity since you are only going from eleven to twelve team members. Is this information correct?

A. Yes, the sponsor is always right.

B. Yes, adding one more person adds only one more communication channel for an eleven-member team.

C. No, Agile teams should be as small as possible.

D. No, adding one more person adds more than one communication channel for an eleven-member team.

2. You are in charge of a software development project that should be completed in 18 months according to the project contract and schedule. The customer has recently faced regulatory changes that require the project to be finished two months earlier, and they ask you to do so. How should you approach this situation?

A. Inform the customer of the impacts of the requirements on project constraints and, after getting the needed approvals, crash the project.

B. Accept the request and cut parts of the project scope to meet the new deadline.

C. Stick to the original schedule and tell the customer that after the contract is signed, the project duration won't change.

D. Cut the duration of all activities across the board for

the project to meet the new requirement.

3. According to the contract, your customer assigned one of their staff to your project office for the purpose of attending meetings and contributing to decision making. The person ends up being too confrontational, and project team members find their behavior intimidating. As project manager, what action should you take in this situation?

A. Ask the customer to replace the person.

B. Unilaterally, decide to isolate the person and don't let them attend project meetings.

C. Since the individual is assigned by the client, you don't have authority over them, so you don't do anything.

D. Confront the individual about their behavior and the impact they are having on the project. Also, tell the customer about the issues.

4. To build the project schedule network diagram, the majority of project management software applications use which of the following methods?

A. Leads and lags.

B. Critical diagramming.

C. Precedence diagramming.

D. Activity-on-arrows diagramming.

5. You are assigned to a new change-driven project. You are working with a team that has never worked together before, but they are experienced with agile techniques. To promote team performance, which of the following techniques are most useful?

A. Creating a detailed schedule with regular

milestones.

B. Allow the team to collaborate and develop a plan to execute the project.

C. Expose and eliminate communication bottlenecks.

D. Create a change control procedure so that only needed changes are addressed and implemented.

6. Which of the following documents is needed to formally authorize a project?

A. Project Statement of Work or SOW.

B. Project Charter

C. Business Case

D. Project Contract

7. You are a project manager about to perform the risk management process. Throughout this process, which of the following documents evolves?

A. Risk Mitigation Plan

B. Contingency Plan

C. Risk Profile

D. Risk Register

8. You are performing scope management processes as the project manager. What function does the WBS Dictionary play?

A. Use it as a glossary to define the acronyms used in the project scope statement.

B. Use to plan for project resources.

C. Used as a glossary to define the acronyms used in the project WBS.

D. Describes the details of each component of the project WBS.

9. You are performing the Control Procurement process for a large project you are managing. Which of the following activities are you least likely to be involved in?

A. Audits

B. Claims Administration

C. Inspection

D. Negotiation

10. Some projects come with a comprehensive procurement phase that includes buying a large number of items. For each item, several suppliers are contracted

for bids. In this project, it is the project manager's responsibility to make sure that every supplier has a clear understanding of the project requirements. For this purpose you can use which of the following techniques?

A. Communication Matrix

B. Formal Presentation

C. One-on-One Discussion

D. Bidder Conferences

11. You are placed in charge of staffing and overseeing a new Scrum project. There are limited resources, and you don't have the budget to hire new people. One person has been pre-assigned to the project and has asked to be the scrum master for the project. While the individual has participated in Scrum projects before, they have never held this role before. What is the best option in this situation?

A. Tell the individual you need someone experienced in the role.

B. Ask the functional manager if they have anyone available to serve as scrum master.

C. Allow the individual to take the role, but require them to enroll in scrum master training right away.

D. Assign the individual coach who has experience as a scrum master.

12. The project manager is reviewing the earned value analysis report performed by the project team. The SPI is 0.87; what does this mean?

A. Your project is running according to budget.

B. The project is getting 87 cents out of each dollar spent.

C. Your project is ahead of schedule.

D. The progress of the project is only 87% of what is planned, so you are behind schedule.

13. A project manager wants a document that shows the work assigned to each member of the project. What's the name of this document?

A. Responsibility Assignment Matrix or RAM.

B. Project Resources Matrix or PRM.

C. Resource Planning Chart or RPC.

D. Project Schedule.

14. You work for a highly cost-sensitive company and are managing a project. You need to reduce costs to the extent possible. Which of the following categories should you consider first for cost reduction?

A. Variable and fixed costs.

B. Indirect and variable costs.

C. Indirect and direct costs.

D. Direct and variable costs.

15. You are tasked with leading an Agile project on a new IT initiative for a company that will have a lot of visibility. For the last several sprints, you've been disappointed with the quality of the product delivered. What is the best option for the team at this point?

A. Ensure transparency of the work progress by using a Kanban board in the team room.

B. Hold more frequent retrospectives.

C. Ensure the team is using test-driven development.

D. Remind the team of the importance of the Agile mindset.

16. Project managers are involved in purchasing various items for projects. If you suddenly receive a letter from the client ordering the immediate termination of the project, what should you do?

A. Refer to Project Closure Guidelines in Organizational Process Assets

B. Perform Inspections and Audits

C. Perform Procurement Audits

D. Release the Project Team

17. Hank has been meeting with stakeholders to determine and understand the requirements for a new project. Which activity is Hank least likely to be involved

in?

A. Inspection

B. Facilitation

C. Questionnaire and Surveys

D. Prototypes

18. Equipment installation for an industrial project can start 15 days after the equipment foundation is finished. What type of dependency is this?          F-S+15

A. Start-to-finish with a 15-day lead.

B. Finish-to-start with a 15-day lag.

C. Finish-to-start with a 15-day lead.

D. Finish-to-finish with a 15-day lag.

19. Which of the following, according to Tuckman, isn't one of the stages of team development?

A. Delegating

B. Performing

C. Forming

D. Norming

20. Abby is the agile team's product owner, and she hires Ben as a software developer for the team. However, after Ben was hired, another project owner reserved 50% of his time for their project. Which of the following is an impact of not having Ben dedicated to Abby's team?

A. Ben may not have the skills for the other team since he wasn't hired with their project in mind.

B. Ben wouldn't be considered a specialist but rather a generalist or T-person.

C. Ben can become dissatisfied because he has too much work to do.

D. Ben's task switching could impact team productivity.

21. While acquiring resources for a project, which activity might a project manager do?

A. Compare labor rates to what is allocated to the project budget.

B. Creating a staffing management plan.

C. Plan communication protocols for virtual team members.

D. Send team members to the training needed for the project.

22. You are starting a new website development project. The team is in the "storming" stage. Several team members are insisting the process occur in a specific way. Other members are unwilling to participate because their views were overruled. To achieve the sponsor's goal of a working prototype in the next few weeks, cooperation and collaboration among the team is key. What is the best action for the project manager to take?

A. Enroll the team in emotional intelligence courses so they learn to be sensitive to the feelings of each other.

B. Hold a team meeting to create a team charter that includes ground rules.

C. Advise the sponsor there may be a delay in delivering the prototype.

D. Hold a networking event so the team members can get to know each other better.

23. You are a project manager in the Control Procurement process. You become aware of the early termination of a contract that is a special case of procurement closure. Special cases of procurement closure can result from everything except which of the following?

A. Convenience of the buyer in the contract.

B. Cause or convenience outside the terminations clause of the contract.

C. Mutual agreement of both parties to terminate.

D. Default of one party.

24. During which process is the cost baseline developed?

A. Develop schedule

B. Determine budget

C. Estimate costs

D. Monitor and control project work

25. Which of the following statements about the project's critical path is true?

A. The critical path always has zero total float, and it shows the earliest possible time to complete a project.

B. The critical path can have zero, positive or negative float.

C. A project only has one critical path.

D. The largest portion of the project budget is used by the critical path compared to other paths.

26. While putting together a project team, you realize that the project charter requires a specific consultant on the team. The consultant has particular knowledge, and

the client has dictated that you hire them as a part of the team. Which tools and techniques of the Acquire Resource process does this situation describe?

A. Multicriteria Decision Analysis

B. Negotiation

C. Pre-Assignment

D. Virtual Team

27. A project manager uses a fishbone diagram to find a project's potential risks. What process is this?

A. Plan Risk Response

B. Control Quality

C. Perform Qualitative Risk Analysis

D. Identify Risk

28. A project manager is currently in the Close Project or Phase process. Which of the following is unnecessary in this situation?

A. Finalizing all activities across all of the Project Management Process Groups.

B. Measuring the project scope against the project management plan.

C. Performing activities such as finalizing open claims, updating procurement records, and archiving information for future use.

D. If a project is terminated before completion, start investigative procedures and document the reason for early termination.

29. You are the project manager on the construction of a stadium for the Winter Olympics. The games start in a month, and there have been weather delays in pouring concrete for the landscaping. Bad weather can affect the quality of the concrete, but since the deadline is closing, you choose not to delay the project and proceed with the remaining concrete work. What risk strategy is this?

A. Transfer

B. Exploit

C. Mitigate

D. Accept

30. Rebecca is the IT manager responsible for a new project. The stakeholders want her to use Scrum, but her team doesn't have the experience. What cultural factor should Rebecca ensure is in place to ensure a successful change to this method?

A. An environment that is safe and transparent.

B. Focus on speed over stability.

C. Emphasize flexibility over predictability.

D. An atmosphere of execution over exploration.

31. Ted is managing a large IT firm's software development project. Based on the essential requirements of the project, Ted wrote an email to one of the functional managers and requested a number of staff to be assigned to the project on a permanent basis for two weeks. The request was rejected. What steps should Ted take next?

A. Raise the issue to higher level managers who determine project priorities.

B. Change the sequence of activities to cope with resource limitations.

C. Record it as a risk in the risk register.

D. Negotiate with the functional manager.

32. You are the project manager for a residential building construction project. The client just requested a change in the lighting system that will increase both risk and costs to the project. What is the first thing you need to do as the project manager?

A. Raise the issue to the project sponsor.

B. Issues a Change Request.

C. Update the project risk register.

D. Analyze the impact of the changes.

33. Which of the following is not attributable to the cost of non-conformance in the Plan Quality Management process?

A. Rework

B. Quality Measures

C. Warranty

D. Downtime

34. As a project progresses, the project team can categorize identified stakeholders to build valuable relationships with the stakeholders. For this purpose, all of the following techniques can be used except which one?

A. Stakeholder cube

B. Stakeholder engagement assessment matrix (SEAM)

C. Salience model

D. Power/Interest grid

35. You are the project manager for a small project in a large organization. Within the organization, a strategic decision was made to shut down one of the operation units that was supposed to work for your project for a few days. This could potentially lead to your project missing a major milestone, so you need to do the necessary planning to acquire outside resources to ensure your project activity is done. For the Plan Risk Response process, which tool and technique will help with this situation?

A. Strategies for positive risk or opportunities.

B. Strategies for negative risk or threats.

C. Contingent response strategies.

D. Risk Reassessment.

36. You are the project manager for an airport construction company. During a project, you realize a

subcontractor is not meeting the quality requirements as set forth in their contract. This risk can result in the final product being rejected by the client. What first step should you take as the manager?

A. Initiate a change request.

B. Perform claim administration.

C. Perform inspection and audit.

D. Raise the risk to the sponsor.

37. Your company has a troubled project, and they put you in charge of performing a financial analysis of the project. The project is on hold, and based on your results, top management will decide between continuing or dropping the project. Which category of costs won't be considered in your analysis?

A. Indirect costs

B. Fixed costs

C. Variable costs

D. Sunk costs

38. You are a project manager in a large organization that has various projects similar to yours. You need to report the project status to top management in a way that will quickly and easily give them the required information. Which of the following reports is the best type to provide the required information to senior management?

A. Project management plans

B. Project detailed schedules

C. Gantt Charts

D. Milestone reports

39. Which of the following is an output from the Acquire Resources process?

A. Organizational chart

B. Project team assignments

C. RAM

D. Staffing management plan

40. Which of the following isn't an input to the Develop Project Charter process?

A. Agreements

B. Business Case

C. Stakeholders Register

D. Organizational Process Assets

41. You are using root cause analysis as a project manager to determine potential risks in your project. Which process best describes the process you are involved in?

A. Plan Quality

B. Identify Risks

C. Control Quality

D. Plan Risk Responses

42. You are assigned a photo transfer project. You meet with the stakeholders and make some observations. The team of seven software developers was given a lot of autonomy in how they conduct their work. The sponsor and business representative are happy with the work so

far, as is evident by the regular feedback on the deliverables. What methodology is the team likely using?

A. Adaptive

B. Predictive

C. Hybrid

D. Waterfall

43. You are working on one of the most visible projects for your company and are several weeks into the project. You are still in the process of meeting with various stakeholders, including suppliers, customers, functional managers, and individual contributors. At some meetings, you hear talk that people aren't pleased with the project and that it is being given high priority. There are some tools that can help you work on this problem. Which of the following is the most appropriate tool to use?

A. Getting feedback through surveys.

B. The stakeholder engagement assessment matrix.

C. The use of ground rules.

D. Preparing and delivering a presentation to the stakeholders on the project benefits.

44. As a project manager, you get the latest project schedule update and realize the project is going to be completed one month after the desired completion date. You have extra resources available, and the activity dependencies are preferential. The project isn't high risk, and the SPI is 0.89. Under these circumstances, what is the best course of action for you as the project manager?

A. Make more activities concurrent.

B. Level the resources.

C. Shift some resources from preferential dependencies

to external ones.

D. Eliminate activities that are of lower importance.

45. In projects, conflicts are unavoidable and common. What are the three most common causes of conflicts in projects?

A. Schedules, Cost, Resources

B. Schedules, Project Priorities, Resources

C. Cost, Resources, Personalities

D. Project Priorities, Resources, Cost

46. You are the project manager for a highly critical project. You get a phone call from the client that they want to have an urgent review meeting about a delay in the delivery of a major piece of equipment for the project. You also find a number of emails from two members of the

team about a conflict that came up this morning. A few minutes later, you get a phone call from one team member while the other comes to your office. Which immediate conflict resolution technique should you use?

A. Collaborating

B. Forcing

C. Compromising

D. Smoothing

47. You were recently assigned a highly critical national project that needs to be finished in a very short amount of time compared to similar projects. You develop the first draft of the project network diagram and see the project can't be finished on time. If you cannot change the network diagram anymore and you have extra human resources, then what would be your best approach?

A. Fast tracking

B. Crashing

C. Risk Analysis

D. Leveling the resources

48. A large company hires you as the project manager and provides you an approved project charter. You know the company undertakes challenging projects, and yours is no exception. What is the first course of action you should take?

A. Plan risk management.

B. Confirm all stakeholders have contributed to the project scope.

C. Identify project risks.

D. Start developing a project management plan.

49. You are the project manager for a large project and also were included in a large part of the procurement activities. You are about to start project closure activities. All final deliverables have been validated. What is the first step in project closure?

A. Start closing contracts.

B. Ensure the completion of scope per the Project Management Plan.

C. Start Claims Administration.

D. Start Administrative Closure.

50. The project you're managing is facing minor delays in the submission of a few deliverables. You are asked to meet with the team in charge of these deliverables. Which tool is best used during the meeting to show the project schedule status to the team members?

A. Gantt Chart

B. Project Network Diagram

C. Milestone Chart

D. Responsibility Assignment Matrix

---

# Answer Key #4

1. D - Adding one more person to the team adds 11 additional communication channels, which can have an impact on complexity. The formula is $N(N-1)/2$ = number of communication channels, with N being the number of team members.

2. A - It is dishonest to arbitrarily trim estimates or scope without directly advising the customer. Simply refusing to make the change is unprofessional.

3. D - The best way to deal with problems is to confront them. Confront the individual about their behavior and notify the customer of the situation. All other actions can be unprofessional and potentially negatively impact the

project.

4. C - Precedence Diagramming or PDM is also known as Activity-on-Node or AON. Most project management and project planning software packages use this method.

5. C - A servant-style leadership is most effective for a team environment that has experience with Agile projects. A characteristic of this style of leadership is to eliminate bottlenecks.

6. B - The project charter is the document that officially authorizes a project and provides authority to the project manager to assign appropriate resources to the project.

7. D - Throughout the risk management process, the risk register is a document that continues to evolve.

8. D - The WBS Dictionary provides detailed descriptions of work packages and their attributes. This includes technical documentation for each WBS element.

9. D - While performing the Conduct Procurements process, negotiation is used. All the other choices are performed during the Control Procurements process.

10. D - Also known as Vendor Conferences, Contractor Conferences or Pre-Bid Conferences. These meetings are between buyers and all prospective sellers before submitting bids or proposals. They are a way to ensure sellers have a clear and common understanding of the procurement and that no one receives preferential treatment.

11. D - Without the budget for new hires and limited resources, you probably won't find someone who is experienced. The most feasible option is to hire an agile coach who can work with the individual throughout the project.

12. D - The SPI is a measure of project performance in terms of the time schedule. A score of less than one means the project is behind schedule.

13. A - A RAM illustrates the association between work packages/activities and members of the project. It allows all team members to view all the project activities that a particular person is assigned to and the level of responsibility.

14. D - Direct costs are related to the project resources, and they can be scaled down or reduced. Variable costs

often depend on the amount of work performed by resources. By reducing the scope and amount of work required, it is a great chance of reducing variable costs.

15. C - Test-driven development is a quality practice that reduces defects. Since the issue is with the quality of the product, this would be the best option.

16. A - Since the project is closing before its completion, the project manager needs to make sure the steps to close the project are followed. The best source of information for this specific situation is the Project Closure Guidelines in Organizational Process Assets.

17. A - The inspection is a technique and tool for the Validate Scope process, while all the other options are used in the Collect Requirements process.

18. B - The dependency between the two is a Finish-to-Start or FS type. Since the second activity can only start after the completion of the first activity, there is a lag time of 15 days before the second activity can start.

19. A - According to Tuckman, the stages of team development are the following: Forming, Storming, Norming, Performing and Adjourning.

20. D - Multitasking between projects affects the whole team's productivity.

21. C - Acquiring resources involves verifying if the costs of selected team members fit within the project budget. If the team consists of virtual team members, special communication protocols need to be implemented to help reduce misunderstanding and conflict.

22. B - The key is that a deliverable is due soon, and the conflicts among the team are putting this goal in jeopardy. The best thing is to have the team agree on ground rules that they can stick to. A team charter will include guidelines, decision-making criteria and communication expectations.

23. B - The rights and responsibilities of both parties in the event of an early termination are covered in the termination clause of the contract. Early termination of a contract is a special case of procurement closure and can occur by mutual agreement of both parties, from one party defaulting, or for the convenience of the buyer if it is provided in the contract.

24. B - During the Determine Budget process, the cost baseline or project budget is developed. This is the

planning process in project cost management.

25. B - A critical path can have a negative total float if there is a constraint set on the project finish date or a positive total float if the project is ahead of schedule. However, the critical path typically has zero float.

26. C - Pre-assignment is the process of selecting project team members in advance. It happens when specific people are promised as a part of the project proposal, the project is dependent on the expertise of a specific person, or staff assignments are defined by the project charter.

27. D - A fishbone diagram is also known as cause and effect analysis or Ishikawa Diagram. They are used in the Identify Risk process to determine potential risks that can affect a project.

28. C - Closing out a contract includes administrative duties. Procurement Close can be done at any stage of the project and isn't associated just with the Close Project or Phase process.

29. D - This situation is an Acceptance strategy. Acceptance is adopted if there is no possibility to

eliminate all threats from a project. This means the team has decided not to change the project management plan to deal with the risk or can't identify a response strategy. The strategy can be active or passive acceptance. Passive acceptance includes no action except documenting the strategy and leaving the team to deal with the risks as they occur. Active acceptance includes establishing a contingency reserve.

30. A - While speed and flexibility are important in agile projects, the most important cultural environment is a safe, honest and transparent environment. Predictive methods encourage an environment that is more execution over exploration.

31. D - Ted has the ultimate responsibility of acquiring resources on time as the project manager. Therefore, he should use the tools and techniques of negotiation to acquire the needed team for the project.

32. D - After receiving a change request, the first thing you want to do is analyze the impacts. Once you compare the impacts, you may need to issue a change request to modify the scope of the project. Raising the issue to the project sponsor may be another option once you are aware

of the impacts of the change.

33. B - The cost of non-conformance results in some form of loss or rejection of the project's output. Quality measures aren't an attribute of non-conformance costs.

34. B - SEAM allows the project team to analyze the variance between the existing and desired engagement levels of the stakeholders and is often used in Plan Stakeholder Engagement. The other three techniques are mapping and categorization techniques used in the Identify Stakeholders process.

35. C - In a situation where the risk response happens after the trigger, some responses are designed to be used only if a specific event occurs. In this case, it is appropriate for the project team to make a response plan that will be executed under predefined conditions.

36. C - The procurement contract specifies inspections and audits required by the buyer and supported by the seller. These can be conducted during the execution of a project to verify compliance with the seller's work processes or deliverables.

37. D - Sunk costs are those expended in the past. They

should not be considered when determining whether or not to continue a project.

38. D - The milestone report is the only one that suits the needs of top management. All the other options are documents that include a lot of redundant or detailed information.

39. B - Project team members are assigned project activities as part of the Acquire Resources process.

40. C - The Develop Project Charter process includes the following inputs: Business Case, Agreements, Enterprise Environmental Factors, and Organizational Process Assets.

41. B - Root cause analysis tools can help identify potential threats based on issues experienced in past incidents. Root cause analysis can be used in both quality management and risk management. However, the situation presented in the question refers only to information-gathering techniques of the Identify Risks process.

42. A - An adaptive culture has the characteristics of a small autonomous team that has earned the trust of

stakeholders. The fact that they are getting regular feedback is also indicative of an iterative, incremental lifestyle being followed.

43. B - SEAM allows you to determine where stakeholders are resistant, neutral, supporting or leading in regards to the project. Based on where you want the stakeholders to be, you can plot strategies to gain support.

44. A - Leveling resources often increases project duration. Removing activities under certain conditions and using the project change process can be a possibility, but since the dependencies are preferential and there are extra resources, the first thing to do is to make more activities concurrent.

45. B - There are seven main sources of conflict in projects: Schedules, Project Priorities, Resource Availability, Technical Opinions, Procedural or Project Administration, Costs, and Personalities. Of these, the top three account for more than 50% of conflicts.

46. D - While collaborating or problem-solving are the best conflict resolution methods, they won't work in this situation. Since you need an immediate technique, smoothing is the best way to resolve things while delaying

conflict resolution.

47. B - Leveling resources often increases project duration. If you can't change the network diagram, then fast-tracking is not a feasible option. Therefore, crashing is the best option to decrease the duration.

48. B - Based on the situation, you weren't involved in the project charter development. This means it is your responsibility to ensure the charter is complete and all of the stakeholders have their input before you move on to the next step of the project planning.

49. B - As project manager, when closing a project, you must review all the previous information from the previous phase closure to ensure all paperwork is completed and that all objectives of the project have been met. The project scope is measured against the scope management plan, so you need to review the scope baseline to ensure completion before you can consider the project closed.

50. A - This tool shows schedule details such as delays, completion and timeline.

# Complete Practice Test

1. You are developing a project management plan for submission to the project sponsor in two weeks. However, the project sponsor wants to review the early resource estimates before the deadline. How are you going to show this information?

A. Work breakdown structure

B. Work breakdown structure dictionary

C. Statement of work

D. Resource breakdown structure

2. A company outsources a project to a supplier; the project has a fixed-price contract. During execution, the supplier agrees to deliver additional customer requirements not included in the original contract. To fulfill the expanded scope, both parties have to add more

resources to keep the project on schedule. Which technique is being used for this project?

A. Fast tracking

B. Crashing

C. Resource leveling

D. Lead and lag

3. If requirements aren't effectively gathered in a scenario where the customer changed the provider for data center implementation after 20% completion, and the new provider project manager requests a meeting with the customer to clarify the impact, what three project areas could be potentially affected?

A. Cost

B. Quality Assurance

C. Schedule

D. Quality Customer Service

E. Quality Planning

4. An organization is undergoing a business transformation. The project manager is assigned to a project related to a new business line. Before defining the project's scope, what should the project manager and team do?

A. Lead a procurement meeting.

B. Create a work breakdown structure.

C. Adapt and tailor existing assets.

D. Sign off on the business case.

5. A project manager is preparing a project's third

progress report and notices the project will experience delays due to late material deliveries. The two previous reports indicated the project was on schedule. What are the next steps the project manager should take?

A. Discuss it with the team to determine the best way to respond.

B. Add it to the issue log and include it in the project report.

C. Contact the procurement manager to expedite material delivery.

D. Escalate the issue to the project owner and ask for a schedule change.

6. What can a project manager do in order to communicate the formal project announcement and relevant information to stakeholders before gaining their commitment?

A. Create a project charter.

B. Conduct a kick-off meeting.

C. Develop the communication management plan.

D. Prepare and distribute the responsible, accountable, consult, and inform RACI matrix.

7. Since the start of a project, the product owner asks about the budget spent for each product iteration during ceremonies. The product owner seems more interested in cost than the product itself. What should the project manager have done to change this behavior?

A. Worked on different estimating approaches to provide confidence in the cost spent on each product increment.

B. Worked on a communications management plan that

included reports of the budget spent in each iteration versus planned to avoid discussions during ceremonies.

C. Worked to clarify the product owner's role in an agile project and the scope of agile ceremonies.

D. Worked to develop a fixed-price contract to switch the focus to value rather than money.

8. A project is aimed at introducing a new business line for an organization through product development in the research and development department. What should the project manager do to increase the chance of success for this project?

A. Start developing a project management plan based on a previous project template from the project management office.

B. Conduct an impact analysis of the new initiative to determine the best way to roll out the project.

C. Plan a working session that focuses on the scope, vision, and mission of the initiative.

D. Determine the business viability of the initiative by conducting benchmarking.

9. During the project setup phase, there was a decline in the attendance of business stakeholders at regular status and daily standup meetings. What action should the project manager take in response?

A. Discuss optional stakeholder representation.

B. Create a communication management plan.

C. Set up a project team room.

D. Hold a project kick-off meeting.

10. In the iteration planning meeting, the team and product owner review user stories. At this time, it is

identified that some high-value stories have more associated risks. What should the agile project manager do?

A. Recommend risky stories be included in early iterations rather than later ones.

B. Recommend the team choose low risk stories for easy completion to keep team motivation high.

C. Work with the product owner to choose stories that should go during the iteration.

D. Use the Pareto analysis to determine which stories can be finished the fastest.

11. After a decision to postpone user testing due to insufficient server capacity and the subsequent procurement of a new service, what steps should a project manager take?

A. Eliminate user testing from the project plan.

B. Use the current server to complete user testing.

C. Request to expedite the new server from the supplier.

D. Wait for the new server's arrival and then reevaluate timelines for user testing.

12. To ensure virtual team meetings are effective, which of the following is best practice?

A. Have the meetings recorded for participants who couldn't attend.

B. Work with the virtual team members to determine the communications most appropriate given their location and participation.

C. Prioritize the agenda with items that require more discussion.

D. Assign a timekeeper and note taker alternating at each meeting.

13. As your project is nearing completion, the project owner and project sponsor get into a struggle regarding who owns the benefits derived from the deliverable. The struggle becomes a matter of litigation. What could you, as the project manager, have done to prevent this conflict from occurring?

A. Identify the project sponsor as a stakeholder at the start of the project.

B. Jointly develop and approve the project charter with both the owner and sponsor.

C. Create a detailed work breakdown structure.

D. Identify and capture any potential issues in the issue log.

14. Which two of the following options will help accelerate a project?

A. Adjust working procedures to streamline and improve efficiency using current resources.

B. Change the critical path by replacing some critical path activities with those that have float.

C. Increase the number of resources to have more people involved so activities get done faster.

D. Rearrange the schedule so some critical path activities can be done concurrently to reduce project duration.

E. Ask resources to work overtime to accelerate the project and get better results.

15. You walk into the project office and find a supplier representative and project team member disagreeing over a clause in the supply agreement. You invite the supplier

for a negotiation with the project team in order to resolve the conflict. Under the principles of negotiation, what should be the aim of the project manager and team?

A. Give up the project objective for a win-lose outcome.

B. Achieve the project objective for a win-lose outcome.

C. Achieve the project objective for a win-win outcome.

D. Achieve the project objective no matter what the outcome.

16. Your project is challenged by many problems that result in defects and stakeholder complaints. You are contemplating a quick and effective approach to address the many problems. Which of the following two actions should you take?

A. Gather the project team members for a

brainstorming session.

B. Refer to organizational process assets or OPAs to assess lessons learned.

C. Use a trend analysis to engage team members.

D. Use an Ishikawa diagram to identify problems.

E. Use a Pareto chart to identify how to address the problems.

17. An influential and unidentified stakeholder appears close to the project completion and jeopardizes the project by withholding approval of closing documents. As project manager, what are two preventative measures you should have taken to avoid this situation?

A. You should have carried out stakeholder identification during the initiation stage of the project.

B. The project owner should have notified you about

the project stakeholders.

C. Identifying and analyzing stakeholders should have been an ongoing task throughout the duration of the project.

D. The stakeholder should have come forward for proper identification at the start of the project.

E. Throughout the project, you should have been creating awareness of the stakeholders' concerns continuously.

18. In what way can a project manager effectively communicate the organizational standards and their unique requirements to stakeholders and project team members?

A. An input to the project management plan will be various external factors of the project, and they will form part of the briefing at the kick-off meeting.

B. Various external factors should already be understood by stakeholders and team members, and including them is optional.

C. Anyone involved in the project must understand the various external factors and make an effort to research them.

D. The stakeholders and team members will be informed about various external factors through the official organizational communications channel.

19. A compliance issue led to an internal audit inspection and caused a delay in the project schedule. What measures could a project manager have proactively taken to prevent this?

A. Ensured that compliance requirements were documented.

B. Create templates to document compliance.

C. Hire a compliance consultant.

D. Engaged stakeholders from the start of the project.

20. In the context of a quality audit conducted for the purpose of quality assurance during the project execution plan, why is the availability of attendance lists important?

A. The document is registered within the lessons learned register.

B. It provides a record that shows the number of attendees in the meeting.

C. It is standard practice on projects to conduct risk review meetings, but attendance is optional.

D. The attendance list is evidence that risk review meetings are held with the appropriate project team members.

21. A vendor's delay in delivering a crucial product solution is impacting the planned release dates. What steps should a project manager take to assist the agile team in dealing with this issue?

A. Work with the vendor to find alternatives.

B. Review and update the release date with the team.

C. Escalate the issue to the functional manager.

D. Have experts and team members work together to find a solution.

22. When a team member suggests a new and quicker method to perform an activity in a hybrid organization and the efficacy is proven by a trusted team member through previous experience, what action should the project manager take?

A. Involve the team member's functional manager.

B. Postpone the decision until the next sprint.

C. Update the work breakdown structure.

D. Assess the impact.

E. Communicate the impact with key stakeholders.

23. You discover a lack of knowledge about local regulations on a new project in an unfamiliar country. As a project manager, what steps should you take?

A. Assign a sufficient budget in case such requirements have to be met.

B. Consult a subject matter expert on how to avoid the requirements.

C. Engage a subject matter expert to see if the

requirements are relevant to the project.

D. Escalate your concerns to the project sponsor.

24. How can you, as the project manager, prevent future situations where a product slated for release fails to meet end-user requirements?

A. Discuss the benefits with the client.

B. Ensure there is a product backlog.

C. Provide examples of similar projects.

D. Hold a session to discuss the deliverable in detail.

25. Local regulators reject the approval of the fiscal metering system due to procedural breaches, leading to increased costs and project delays. What steps could the project manager take to avoid this scenario?

A. Refer to lessons learned from previous projects.

B. Notify stakeholders of the factory acceptance tests for meters.

C. Ensure compliance with the stakeholder requirements.

D. Revise the stakeholder engagement plan.

26. Now that government regulation has brought it to light, what should a project manager do about a missing feature in a completed artifact?

A. Create a user story and add it to the next sprint.

B. Review the product roadmap.

C. Review backlog items during sprints.

D. Reference and update the definition of done.

27. At the start of a new project, what steps can a project manager take to ensure the team's adoption of an agile approach?

A. Perform a skills assessment of the team.

B. Advocate the use of agile techniques.

C. Engage only resources who are comfortable using agile.

D. Hire agile consultants to lead the team.

28. A competitor announces a similar product launch in the market one week into your agile project. What is the next step you should take?

A. Ensure the product backlog will deliver the minimum valuable product first.

B. Immediately cancel the sprint and start a new sprint once you determine the requirements for the next sprint.

C. Hire a subject matter expert from the competitor company to consult.

D. Ask the team members to continue with the delivery and address the issue at the retrospective.

29. You are faced with frequent complaints about project performance from the customer despite sending sprint velocity and results reports via email. What steps can you take to address this issue?

A. Involve the customer in sprint planning and review sessions to agree on release dates.

B. Schedule regular sessions with the customer to explain reports and address feedback.

C. Send a document to the customer detailing the team capacity and role assignments.

D. Have the technical leader call the customer to explain the technical details regarding project issues.

30. As a project manager, what should you do to handle the failure to upgrade the older system halfway through the upgrade process?

A. Abandon the old system and encourage the team to speed up the project since there is nothing more to do.

B. Ask for time to restore the old system while continuing with the project.

C. Assess the impact with the functional manager to tell key stakeholders about mitigation plans and seek approval.

D. Encourage the team to continue working since the project manager isn't responsible for the old system, but keep checking the baseline.

31. You are the project manager on a government software project, with the director serving as the project owner. What steps do you need to take to address the director's lack of engagement and ensure regular feedback on project artifacts?

A. Review responsibilities and determine communication preferences.

B. Obtain alternative feedback from the customer.

C. Recommend an open-door policy for the project.

D. Adopt a collaborative approach.

32. To alleviate the client's worries about a delay in a long-term project, what two steps should the project manager take?

A. Create a baseline schedule.

B. Review the change control process.

C. Add more resources to critical path tasks.

D. Perform a risk reserve analysis.

E. Run some activities concurrently.

33. You are contracted to manage a project for a startup with grants from a foreign source. Midway through the project, you are informed that a government regulatory requirement might affect the project because of the foreign funding sources. If all necessary approvals for the project have been received, what should you do?

A. Determine ownership of the project based on the approved project charter and continue with the project.

B. Consult the risk register to determine the likelihood of the project being accepted by the customer and meet regulatory requirements.

C. Confirm that the project is in compliance with regulations and stay aware of all legal implications.

D. Stop the project, ask for additional funds for work permits, and continue without further delays.

34. You are in the middle of completing an IT project when two project team members discover a new feature that will change how the product appears and make it more appealing aesthetically. They approach you to approve the addition to the deliverables, which will increase client satisfaction and possibly increase the chance of getting additional project contracts from the client. How should you respond?

A. Approve the idea to achieve the projected expectations of team members.

B. Remind the team members that without an approved change request, the focus should only be on the agreed scope.

C. Get the buy-in from the remaining team members and implement the feature once you have consent.

D. Implement the change as soon as possible to potentially improve future revenue.

35. During the product's current iteration, the stakeholder is unavailable during the review, and there is a lack of input. What steps can you take as the project manager to ensure the stakeholder is satisfied with the new features?

A. Wait for all stakeholder's approval before implementing the changes.

B. Ensure that updated project information is always accessible to all stakeholders.

C. Meet individually with all stakeholders to avoid any disagreement.

D. Schedule meetings only when all stakeholders can

be present.

36. What steps should you take as the project manager to address the situation where a critical project deliverable has not been resolved even though several weeks of troubleshooting have happened? The team is blaming the technical challenge and their lack of knowledge for the issue.

A. Escalate the issues to a functional manager to bring a technical expert to the team.

B. Explain the situation to the customer and include an action plan.

C. Keep the team focused on the sprint backlog to accomplish the next release milestone.

D. Update the risk and issue logs, including the action plan to resolve the issue.

E. Establish a new release date for the deliverable with

the product owner.

37. How would you provide initial estimations for timelines, costs, and unforeseen product challenges when you don't have past data or historical records for the new technology deployment project?

A. Develop up-front project management plans and include a detailed budget.

B. Provide guidance on project cost, time, and quality.

C. Develop estimations with your team and explain the assumptions to the client.

D. Encourage the team to perform retrospectives at intervals.

38. You are working in an organization using a hybrid project delivery method. You are tasked with

implementing a new human resources system where another project is delivering the infrastructure component as part of a business transformation program, but the project manager of the infrastructure project can't provide delivery dates, which is necessary for finalizing the project schedule?

A. Wait for the infrastructure project to have a schedule and then develop the human resources system project's schedule.

B. Discuss the situation with the other project manager, agree on some milestones, and continue working on the human resources system project's schedule.

C. Develop a schedule based on the information available from the management team and then progressively align milestones with the infrastructure project.

D. Develop a schedule based on the information available and ask the other project manager to align the infrastructure milestones with the delivery dates of the human resource project.

39. At what point in an agile project should you, as the project manager, engage stakeholders?

A. At the beginning of the project.

B. At the close of the project.

C. When you encounter challenges in the project.

D. Throughout the life cycle of the project.

40. A key third-party supplier offers discounted client services and expresses concerns over inadequate return on investment. As project manager, what can you do to address this issue and prevent risks to the project?

A. Engage in negotiations with the third-party supplier

for additional compensation.

B. Highlight the binding nature of the contract to the supplier.

C. Investigate alternative third-party suppliers that have comparable services.

D. Consult the stakeholders to reach a consensus on a plan that will resolve the issue.

41. Due to illness, a team member is taking a week off. They are currently responsible for a task on the critical path. What is the next step you should take as the project manager?

A. Choose another team member to immediately take over the task.

B. Evaluate the potential impacts of a project delay.

C. Refer to the risk response plan to mitigate the issue.

D. Convince the team member to complete the task.

42. You are implementing a phase of an IT project in a location prone to security issues. A team member working at a remote site notifies you that a permit fee was not received by the local regulatory agency involved. However, you are certain the fee was paid. The team member reminds you that a test on the critical path is scheduled for that location on the same day. What should you do as the project manager?

A. Request payment evidence from the team member from the project management office and ensure the hard copy payment receipt is delivered to the regulatory agency, then wait for feedback.

B. Request a meeting with the agency officer to provide payment evidence and verify the consequences of delayed payment to ensure the test proceeds as planned.

C. Instruct the team member to proceed with the test because the penalty for non-compliance with the permit has a negligible cost impact, and you can't alter the test.

D. Instruct the team member to proceed with the test to avoid a lag in the critical path and the test can't be delayed further, and the fee was paid.

43. As project manager, you get word that your firm has been taken over by a rival when you are mid-fifth sprint of a significant product development project that the new company already has a similar product of, coinciding with the start of the product release. What should be your immediate next step as the project manager?

A. Compare both products' use, features and other factors through product analysis.

B. Work with the project manager in charge of a similar project on product activities.

C. Request support from the sponsor and comply with established change management processes.

D. Compile a report on the project completion and record key takeaways.

44. You are the project manager leading a cross-functional team and you discover during a brainstorming session that resistance to change by some team members is hindering the overall performance of the team. What should you do?

A. Clearly articulate the goals of the project to the team.

B. Request that the project sponsor review the project charter and offer support.

C. Encourage the team members to voice their concerns and work towards getting their commitment to the project.

D. Conclude the brainstorming session and consider alternative methods like individual interviews.

45. As project manager, you are tasked with overseeing a project aimed at incorporating agile principles into the organization. You are currently developing the definition of the project's scope. What is the first thing you should do?

A. Assess the scope, determine necessary outcomes, and establish backup plans for recognized risks.

B. Conduct a workshop with the project owner and the project team to establish the product backlog and acceptance criteria.

C. Establish a communication platform to share the scope definition and product backlog with the project team.

D. Meet with the project team to define essential requirements.

46. Due to a significant shift in government policy, the completion date for a project may be postponed. The project is currently 90% finished. As project manager, what should you do next?

A. Suspend the project until the government policy issue is resolved.

B. Engage the change control board to assess possible impacts to the project.

C. Move forward with the project since it is nearly complete.

D. Assign a new completion date for the project and inform the stakeholders.

47. As a project manager, what should you use to calculate the duration of a project as a part of project scheduling?

A. Collaborate with your team to formulate a comprehensive release plan.

B. Use stories in the project to estimate the duration.

C. Inquire with the project sponsor about their desired completion date.

D. Ensure that the resources are fully dedicated to the project.

48. As project manager you have concerns about the outcome of a hybrid project due to a change in a competitor's products and services that may make the project deliverables outdated once complete. However, senior management is not authorized by the project manager to either reduce the project's scope or diminish the result's quality. What can you do to successfully deliver the project?

A. Perform a business impact assessment, utilize unconventional materials, and reduce the number of skilled resources in order to control costs.

B. Evaluate the effect the change will have on the project timeline and request approval from the change control board.

C. Maintain the current timeline, request additional funds from management, and avoid modifying the project scope.

D. Terminate the project and start a new one since you can't alter the project scope and quality.

49. Six months ago, a company was awarded a two-year project. The procurement process hasn't started. What steps should be taken to advance the project?

A. Prepare the procurement management plan for the project.

B. Assemble the team to create a procurement management plan.

C. Monitor the procurement process based on the organization's procurement management guidelines.

D. Elevate the issue to higher-level management.

50. How should a project manager handle issues in an agile project if a team member raises concerns regarding health and safety concerning the project outcome?

A. Share sufficient health and safety documentation with the customer.

B. Escalate the concern to the health and safety division.

C. Develop a comprehensive health and safety policy for the company.

D. Make sure the definition of done incorporates the necessary health and safety requirements.

51. The project for an IT contract requires that all team members have IT security certification. As a project manager, you learn that one team member has fabricated their certificate. What should be your first step to handle this situation?

A. Update the project management plan to include the resources needed to get the team member certified.

B. Update the issue log and remove the team member from the project team.

C. Ensure the remaining team members have valid certificates.

D. Investigate why this issue wasn't discovered earlier.

52. The project team has completed the project deliverable and passed the acceptance criteria. Which of the following statements confirms that project benefits have been achieved?

A. The deliverable is approved, and the value is confirmed.

B. The deliverable solved all issues specified by the project sponsors.

C. There have been some improvements in the ability to make decisions.

D. The project was completed on schedule without end-user complaints.

53. You are the project manager overseeing a virtual team from different countries working remotely in different time zones. Team members are failing to meet deadlines and deliver expected results due to poor communication. How should you resolve this issue?

A. Provide a deliverables list to the team to guide them.

B. Engage with team members to understand the challenges.

C. Organize time management training for the team members.

D. Take steps to co-locate the team into the same office.

54. Your project team is in the planning stage of a challenging project with a novel project and a set deadline. The project sponsor is seeking a comprehensive schedule, but the team is challenged to estimate task timing due to dependencies on other business units. As the project manager, what life cycle methodology should you use in the solution of this issue?

A. A hybrid life cycle with a prioritized product backlog that is approved by the sponsor.

B. A predictive life cycle that features a schedule agreed upon by all relevant business units.

C. An Agile approach that features a comprehensive schedule agreed upon by all relevant business units.

D. An iterative process with task duration estimates and a budget approved by the project sponsor.

55. A hybrid project is underway with multiple stakeholders. Following the PMO's instructions, project status reports and related documents are centralized in the repository. During a review, the project manager observes that certain documents need to be updated or included. What should be done in this situation?

A. Consult with the project sponsor to minimize documentation.

B. Collaborate with team leaders to keep necessary reports current.

C. Pause all project operations until the updated documents are placed in the repository.

D. Arrange for a knowledge transfer session.

56. The company leadership is closely monitoring the project's iteration as it transitions from a predictive to a hybrid predictive-agile method. They closely follow-up with the project manager because of concerns over the realization of benefits and to guarantee the project's success. What should the project manager do?

A. Provide regular updates on the progress, benefits, and potential risks.

B. Present the project's business value and secure leadership support.

C. Provide a low-benefit analysis report.

D. Proactively share progress updates with the leadership team and provide them with clear and quantifiable reports of the benefits realized in each iteration.

57. The core project team works remotely from the project advisory team. This requires a continuous information exchange and approval of project documents by both teams. Any approval delays incur additional expenses. Which of the following methods ensures the project manager has all necessary, current and adequately approved documents?

A. Facilitate a discussion to determine the appropriate Configuration Management System.

B. Implement a change management system.

C. Allow the core and advisory teams to establish and keep document classification and labeling systems.

D. Have the sponsor manage and approve changes in a centralized document repository.

58. You are the project manager of a culturally diverse

team. While executing a project, the team encounters significant disagreements. What should you do?

A. Deal promptly with conflicts through open communication and agreement on common objectives.

B. Let the team handle differences initially.

C. Investigate the source of the disagreement.

D. Get the team involved in team-bonding activities.

59. An agile project team needs help managing the changes made to a product because of a complicated and prone-to-mistake process. What actions should the project manager take?

A. Implement a streamlined change management process that reduces the risk of errors.

B. Evaluate the efficiency of the process during the

upcoming retrospective meeting and decide if modifications are needed.

C. Abolish the agile process and revert to a traditional project management approach.

D. Facilitate a discussion to determine the root cause.

60. You are the project manager who is starting a new agile project. You work in an organization where virtual teams are normal. With this setup, challenges frequently arise. As project manager, what steps should you take to support the team in overcoming these challenges?

A. Perform strengths, weaknesses, opportunities, and threats analysis to identify the status of the team and take quick and appropriate action.

B. Gather a team to address the new challenges immediately.

C. Delay addressing the challenges until the next daily

scrum meeting so you can inform the entire team.

D. Collaborate with the project owner to determine the best plan of action for the team to overcome the challenges.

61. A project team that often completes backlog items within a four-week sprint is facing an issue with a crucial team member being absent for a week and unable to complete their ongoing tasks. What action should a project manager take?

A. Remove some items from the current sprint with agreement from the product owner.

B. Reassign unfinished tasks to other team members.

C. Facilitate a discussion between the product owner and the team to find a solution.

D. Add a temporary resource to the team in order to finish work on time.

62. A client's relationship with the project team is characterized by negative and hostile interactions. This leads to a situation where team members aren't willing to continue their involvement in the project. What should a project manager do?

A. Schedule a meeting with the client to discuss the concerns.

B. Facilitate a discussion with the project team to set the client's expectations.

C. Negotiate using open communication, clear expectations, and mutually beneficial solutions.

D. Involve all team members in a stakeholder engagement.

63. A new product development project has been initiated and needs investors. It is your responsibility to

convince some crucial investors, but they need information before making investment decisions. What should you do?

A. Provide a detailed analysis of the market, project scope, timeline, budget, risks, benefits, and expected outcomes.

B. Prepare and present a cost-benefit analysis.

C. Assess and describe all the risks associated with product development and launch, then present a detailed risk management plan to the stakeholders.

D. Plan development activities to engage the stakeholders in various project phases.

64. A company is facing market changes so they rush the product release schedule from yearly to quarterly. As the project manager, you see this as a chance to implement an agile life cycle, but upper management isn't convinced. What can you do to enhance the success

potential of using this approach?

A. Provide a comprehensive presentation to upper management on the benefits of using an agile life cycle.

B. Present the product backlog with the product roadmap.

C. Delay implementing the agile life cycle until upper management is on board with the situation.

D. Have the team work virtually and use cost savings to speed up delivery.

65. You are leading a project where a former low-level stakeholder has been recently promoted to a high-level role. What actions should you take to guarantee the appropriate participation of the new high-level stakeholder?

A. Update the Communications Management Plan.

B. Update the Stakeholder Engagement Plan.

C. Update the Resource Management Plan.

D. Update the Risk Management Plan.

66. During the last sprint review, there were conflicting opinions. The product owner asserts that the product doesn't deliver any value. The project manager believes it meets all the specifications. This confuses the team. When using a hybrid approach, what should the project manager do?

A. Review the project's benefits management plan with the product owner.

B. Escalate the matter to the executive board.

C. Ask the development team to prioritize the project backlog.

D. Using appropriate conflict resolution techniques to solve the conflict.

67. What should a project manager do to mitigate the negative impact of the new regulation with a deadline approaching on an upcoming project that is essential to the organization's annual goals and carries the risk of hefty fines for non-compliance?

A. Evaluate the consequences of not starting the project and communicate the results to the relevant stakeholders.

B. Outsource the tasks with a higher risk level to a third party.

C. Secure additional financial resources to accommodate the cost of external services as needed.

D. Create simulations, prototypes, and models to better understand potential outcomes.

68. What two solutions should a project manager implement to address the recurring retrospective action item that involves verifying and validating delivery functionality before production readiness?

A. Adjust the team's velocity to account for extra testing.

B. Integrate unit and test criteria into the validation process.

C. Shift delivery methodology to test-driven development.

D. Re-examine acceptance criteria in the working agreement with the project team.

69. Collaboration and support are needed from cross-functional business teams across different functional areas on a massive transformation project. The project manager should follow what two steps in order to ensure the thorough completion of the stakeholder register?

A. Divide the project into domain areas.

B. Finalize the stakeholder register through team discussions.

C. Assess the interests, influence, and impact of stakeholders and compile the stakeholder register through team discussions.

D. Seek recommendations from the business sponsor or senior leadership.

E. Reach out to potential stakeholders and inquire about their interest in the project.

70. To ensure effective collaboration among a geographically dispersed team on a hybrid project without incurring high costs while navigating the financial constraints of a new company, what should be the project manager's priority?

A. Ensure the team has access to and is trained on appropriate virtual collaboration tools.

B. Consider reorganizing project tasks to take advantage of the team member's physical proximity to each other.

C. Reevaluate the project budget to identify areas where cost savings can be achieved, then redirect the savings towards team co-location.

D. Form the team from one location since the new approach needs co-location.

71. To ensure key stakeholders receive the necessary information and are fully prepared for the status meetings during the incremental approach of an innovation project, what should the project manager implement to avoid further complaints about a lack of preparation for the meetings?

A. Share updated information with key stakeholders

the day before each meeting.

B. Work with the key stakeholders to determine the meeting agenda and share it with them before each meeting.

C. Hold pre-meeting discussions with key stakeholders as needed.

D. Provide a clear and detailed project status report to the key stakeholders one week before the meeting.

72. When a new team member expresses frustration about their inability to complete a task despite putting in a lot of effort, what is the first step a project manager needs to take?

A. Provide support and guidance to the team member.

B. Determine the underlying reason for the difficulty and find a solution.

C. Assign a mentor to the team member.

D. Evaluate the team member's performance and address any needed improvements.

73. In Location A, the project manager has a team of local and remote members, including developers and a quality assessor in separate remote locations. This geographical separation can cause a lag in communication and hinder the ability of the team to effectively collaborate and communicate. What can the project manager implement to minimize the impact of the communication lag and improve the ability of the team to effectively work together?

A. Daily video conferences.

B. Assign a dedicated team member to handle communication between the remote locations.

C. Create a fishbowl window.

D. Limit communication between team members to essential updates only.

74. To ensure a smooth project initiation, what should a project manager prioritize, given the presence of a team member known for challenging organizational procedures and processes?

A. Hold a meeting with the team to examine the organizational process assets and establish guidelines for the project.

B. Request the project sponsor clarify and distribute the guidelines to all members of the team.

C. Suggest the project sponsor replace or remove the problematic team member.

D. Schedule a session with the team member to analyze the project management plan.

75. To enhance performance in a company with difficulties transitioning to hybrid project management, what actions should a project manager take?

A. Assign tasks to team members and then closely monitor their progress.

B. Provide training on hybrid practices and hold coordination meetings.

C. Create performance reports for team members to review and take action.

D. Develop a work breakdown structure and RACI chart to clarify responsibilities and tasks.

76. To address communication difficulties in a large organization with team members and functional leaders expressing concerns about being informed too late or not being included in project discussions, what is the most effective approach for the project manager to take?

A. Follow the established process set forth in the communication plan.

B. Provide regular email updates to each functional manager on the status of the project and next steps.

C. Organize a meeting with team leaders to come up with a solution.

D. Check the RACI chart for information on who needs to know what and when to ensure compliance.

77. As the project manager, you are responsible for supplying hardware and software components for an integrated project. You are given a Gantt chart with customer approval for the product development timeline. The software development team wants to employ agile methods. In this situation, what is your best course of action?

A. Evaluate the most suitable project method to maximize business value.

B. Consider implementing agile sprints within the established timeline.

C. Follow the customer-approved Gantt chart and advise the team to do the same.

D. Examine the customer's involvement and decide on the appropriate method.

78. To address the issue of newly arising tasks and dependencies during project execution, impeding progress and causing uncertainty about decision-making responsibilities, what action should the project manager take?

A. Implement an RACI chart to clarify task accountability among the project team members.

B. Use a Gantt chart to track progress towards key

milestones.

C. Engage the sponsors to determine decision-making responsibilities.

D. Apply a work breakdown structure to ensure all project requirements are accounted for.

79. As a project manager, what steps should you take before adding a new team member during the execution phase of a project to reduce its impact on project performance?

A. Update the social agreement with the existing team members to avoid misunderstandings.

B. Explain the social agreement to the new team member for clarity on rules and expectations.

C. Communicate the social agreement to all team members for feedback and to encourage a positive environment.

D. Explain social contract rules to the new team member to ensure understanding of responsibilities.

80. A team member requests the project manager's intervention when another team member repeatedly modifies their deliverable in each sprint. What should the project manager do?

A. Speak with the team member to determine the reason for the changes.

B. Discuss the issue of deliverable ownership with both team members to resolve the conflict.

C. Review the scope management plan and ensure all team members are following established processes.

D. Facilitate a meeting to address the issue and find a resolution for both parties.

81. As a project manager, you are faced with a situation where the performance of a critical subsystem is uncertain, and the success of the project is at risk. Two technical alternatives were identified, but it is uncertain if either will perform satisfactorily. What is the first thing you should do?

A. Direct the project team to assess and evaluate the alternatives for the subsystem.

B. Add subsystem performance to the issue log and assign an owner for the issue.

C. Schedule work for the most promising of the two alternatives.

D. Implement a risk response plan to mitigate the impact on the project.

82. As the project manager, you identify that a key team member lacks the necessary skills to fulfill their assigned task, and you are still early on in the project.

What is the best way to address this issue?

A. Incorporate training into the resource management plan to improve the abilities of team members.

B. Talk with the team member about their training requirements and identify any gaps.

C. Review each task with the team members as they start to ensure understanding and competence then provide ongoing support.

D. Escalate the issue to the functional manager for a solution.

83. A project is experiencing delays due to a lack of response from a senior executive. What should the project manager do?

A. Develop a plan to send regular reminders to the

senior executive to ensure a prompt response.

B. Rework the project schedule to exclude the task that is causing a delay and impact on the critical path.

C. Use personal connections to reach out to the senior executive to get a response.

D. Inform the senior executive's superior about the delays and seek intervention.

84. The organization has chosen to shift from a predictive approach to an agile approach and mandated that all projects must adopt the agile approach. To ensure the benefits of this transition are achieved, what steps should the project manager take?

A. Hold regular team standup meetings to assess the realization of benefits.

B. Ensure the benefits management plan aligns with the product backlog for the project.

C. During sprint demonstrations, review the benefits management plan.

D. Assign the scrum master the responsibility for setting up the benefits management plan in the next team standup.

85. A team member was assigned to work on a specific task in a six-month project. In the fifth month, the team member leaves the project to pursue another job opportunity. What next step should the project manager take in this situation?

A. Discuss the issue with the team member to ensure he finishes his work in the notice period.

B. Verify the terms of the team member's contract to properly terminate his project involvement.

C. Assess what remaining project work will be impacted and ensure there are sufficient resources in place to continue the work.

D. Examine the contingency plan for the project to identify if additional resources can be obtained to hire a replacement team member to complete the remaining tasks.

86. You are the project manager for a complex project that involves multiple disciplines. You choose to assign specific project management tasks to various team members. In this scenario, what is the best course of action for you to take?

A. Create a communications management plan for the project and share it with all stakeholders involved in the project.

B. Create a mentorship plan and include it in regular project status reports.

C. Develop a hierarchical representation of the project organization and a detailed description of the project scope.

D. Establish a RACI chart to clarify roles and responsibilities among project team members.

87. Within the healthcare industry, the country recently revised its safety regulations. What action should you take first as the project manager?

A. Review the potential impacts of the revised regulations on the project.

B. Update the risk register to reflect the newly emerged risks.

C. Get input from the stakeholders, including the human resources department, to develop an updated health and safety procedure plan.

D. Use the project risk management process to evaluate options and determine the best action to take.

88. Your project team has successfully achieved a milestone, and you observe the team members have demonstrated exceptional performance. What communication approach should you adopt to convey your recognition of their efforts?

A. Send a group email that recognizes and appreciates their performance.

B. Wait until the end of the project to celebrate.

C. Hold a team meeting to formally acknowledge the team's performance.

D. Execute a reward system.

89. As a project manager, you plan the next release based on the last two release learnings. The product backlog is refined for the next release. What can help you determine the time frame for the upcoming release?

A. Retrospective notes, product roadmap, and test cases.

B. Burndown chart, product backlog, and retrospective notes.

C. WBS, product roadmap, and resource calendar.

D. Business requirement document and user stories.

90. You are a newly appointed project manager joining an existing team with strong personalities that have caused performance problems, leading to higher management involvement. What is the first step you should take?

A. Immediately implement a plan to resolve conflicts.

B. Assess team dynamics and observe interactions.

C. Facilitate the team to form the work agreement.

D. Hold on to one session with the strongest

personalities.

91. A company with a long history of predictive methods is looking to integrate some iterative initiatives into the project framework. A project manager has been appointed to spearhead the initial project in the new hybrid environment. To raise awareness and understanding of the hybrid approach throughout the organization, what steps should the project manager take?

A. Hold a project team meeting to clarify team roles and responsibilities.

B. Through iterative sessions, develop project timelines and keep stakeholders informed.

C. Include stakeholders in project review sessions and daily stand-ups.

D. Suggest senior management go through iterative methodology training.

92. There is friction between members of a multidisciplinary team; what next step should the project manager take to address the issue?

A. Identify team members and review their performance.

B. Consult with the sponsor to find replacement team members.

C. Evaluate the issue and apply appropriate conflict resolution techniques.

D. Report the issue in the monthly project executive summary.

93. The project team is frustrated with the compliance department, which keeps adding documentation and process requirements that impact the team's desired work style. The team asks you, as the project manager, to step

in; what should you do to address this issue?

A. Educate the team on the significance of compliance with project goals and creating value.

B. Advice the compliance department to streamline the documentation process so the team can focus on delivering value.

C. Designate a time each day to review compliance requirements and complete necessary tasks.

D. Include the compliance department in daily standup meetings to prevent misunderstandings and conflicts between the groups.

94. The product owner asks to demonstrate the completed functionality to key product stakeholders. The project is in its early days and has only finished three iterations. This will be the stakeholders' first exposure to an agile project. What actions should the project manager take?

A. Educate key stakeholders about the agile project approach and set expectations for the demo of completed functionality.

B. Remind the product owner that communication and stakeholder management is their responsibility.

C. Prepare stakeholders for the demo of limited functionality along with requirements and prototypes.

D. Provide a direct link to the UAT environment to reduce distractions for the team.

95. What should a project manager do to create an archetype user for a new software project aimed at a specific niche of university students?

A. Use Persona

B. Use a survey to get an idea of the user

C. Contract with an architectural firm

D. Publish a marketing plan

96. Before a product release, there is a conflict between two team members, and the team needs to work together to complete the project. What initial steps should a project manager take to resolve the conflict and ensure a smooth completion of the project?

A. Use an agile coach to educate the team on resolving conflicts without risking the project.

B. Assess the team members' interactions and discuss their concerns before implementing a conflict resolution strategy.

C. Schedule meetings with HR and team members to emphasize the significance of the upcoming product delivery.

D. Advise team members they are delaying progress by

conflicting rather than focusing on delivering a functional product.

97. You are a project manager assuming control of a project from a previous project manager who had a commanding management style. You observe that a senior supervisor's morale is low. What steps should you take to address this issue?

A. Increase authority.

B. Identify the cause of the moral issue.

C. Update the issue log.

D. Propose a reward system.

98. The audit team, during a project execution, determined that critical regulatory requirements weren't being met. What should have been the first step to avoid

this problem?

A. Update the issue log with regulatory requirements.

B. Assess the internal and external regulatory environments.

C. Have the audit team review the project management plan.

D. Include a member of the audit team on the project.

99. A project is almost complete, and a stakeholder wants to know how the outcomes will impact the organization. What should be reviewed with the stakeholders?

A. Business case.

B. Benefits management plan.

C. Project charter.

D. Assumption log.

100. What should a project manager do to ensure a newly formed team, including junior members with no prior experience, work together effectively on the correct items during the sprint as requested by the product owner?

A. Dedicate time during the project to coach team members on the required skills.

B. Highlight the importance of prioritizing the sprint backlog to the team and product owner.

C. Implement Scrum practices to enhance productivity.

D. Ensure effective communication of project information and progress updates.

101. During a retrospective meeting, the project team expressed concerns that unresolved issues from previous iterations are having a negative impact on their progress. What can the project manager do to enhance productivity?

A. Ensure the project team attends daily standup meetings to discuss impediments.

B. Document the issues in the issue log and wait to solve them later.

C. Extend the daily standup meetings to further discuss the issues.

D. Escalate the issue to the project sponsor to get the issues solved immediately.

102. A project team spread out across different locations is facing challenges in collaborating between co-located and remote teams. This has led to a decline in productivity. What can the project manager do to resolve these issues?

A. Require team members to work from a single location.

B. Secure outside experts to provide guidance to the team.

C. Establish procedures for resolving conflicts.

D. Organize in-person meetings for the project team.

103. An innovative project is using AI to identify chemical compounds for the development of new products. The project needs to deliver at least one product specification within two months and has a fixed budget that can't be increased. The duration of AI processing can range from three days to two weeks, and the findings can't be predicted. How can the project manager maximize the business value delivered with the remaining budget?

A. Ensure the specification iterations are limited to 50% of the overall duration.

B. Ensure the AI processing is limited to 25% of the overall budget.

C. Plan an iteration immediately after AI processing to analyze and prioritize the development goals.

D. Plan the specification work as a predictive task with a fixed duration to guarantee value.

104. As a project manager, what steps would you take to handle the potential termination of a multi-million dollar, multi-year product development project that is 70% complete? The project is being terminated because of unacceptable deliverables and execution. The vendor is willing to perform re-work without penalty, but the relationship is strained.

A. Request the customer's approval for re-work since the vendor possesses specialized product knowledge.

B. Agree on a revised definition of done with the customer, with the vendor covering the expenses of the re-work.

C. Facilitate between the vendor and customer to negotiate acceptance criteria.

D. Tell the vendor to perform re-work since they failed to meet the necessary standards.

105. If a stakeholder expresses concern about an initiative not delivering value to the organization at the start of a project, how can the project manager increase the chances of the project's success?

A. Review the business case and benefits management plan.

B. Provide constant communication of the project status to the stakeholders.

C. Schedule training for everyone on using the new

product.

D. Perform an audit to ensure the benefits are realized.

106. As the project manager, what can you do to ensure the missing key deliverable is included and the intended project value is delivered in the existing complex project?

A. Escalate the deliverable issue to the project sponsor.

B. Confirm the expected deliverables and re-baseline the project.

C. Track it through the requirements traceability matrix.

D. Use the contingency fund for more resources to complete the missing deliverable.

107. A new product owner needs help prioritizing product requirements; what steps should a project

manager take?

A. Assign the task of prioritization to the development team.

B. Coach, the owner, on prioritizing product specifications.

C. Prioritize product backlog for the owner.

D. Request the owner to undergo training in agile prioritization.

108. A project is on track for completion in three weeks. Two key team members approach the project manager about a disagreement on the process for finishing the final task and believe their method can have a major improvement. The project manager chooses to stick to the current process while considering implementing the improved strategy for future projects. What approach to conflict resolution is this?

A. Collaborative/Problem Solve

B. Compromise/Reconcile

C. Force/Direct

D. Smooth/Accommodate

109. During a review meeting, the project manager learns unclear requirements may impact the scheduled completion of the project. The project sponsor still requests completion by the original deadline. Using agile practices, how should the project manager approach this issue?

A. Recommend delivery in multiple releases with a focus on the known scope and important functionalities.

B. Inform the sponsor that you'll add a change request for the scope at the next iteration.

C. Log the issue as the unclear scope and escalate it to the product owner to make a decision on the unclear requirements.

D. Ask the scrum master to clarify the scope before the project continues.

110. The Scrum team realizes that work has consistent spillover during the last several sprints because of a bottleneck in the code review task that resulted from an external expert and creates a dependency on the team. What is the first step the project manager should take?

A. Assess and highlight the bottleneck, then increase the sprint length.

B. Assess the capability of the team and identify the internal training required to remove the bottleneck.

C. Arrange an alternative to have a backup expert in order to avoid spillover.

D. Work along with the team, start reviewing the code and stop reviews from the expert in order to avoid spillover.

111. To develop a hybrid approach for a project, the project manager needs to assess the organizational culture. The project manager needs to balance X and Y, where X and Y represent two key factors that need to be considered when evaluating the organizational culture.

A. Exploration and Stability

B. Speed and Traditional Models

C. Flexibility and Predictability

D. Disruption and Conformity

112. A stakeholder requests to present the ROI and all new commercial value of the project to the executive

board during the final stages of a project. What should the project manager do in response to this request?

A. Present the cost-benefit analysis.

B. Present the achieved benefits.

C. Present the cost management plan.

D. Present the financial success factors.

113. The internal compliance department requests an approved requirements document. The project team uses an agile approach with user stories to capture requirements. What is the process for meeting this request?

A. Discuss the project approach with the compliance department to address their request and align with the control objective.

B. Compile all user stories into a document, then obtain approval from the product owner once the project is completed.

C. Assign the compliance requirement to the product owner on the project's Kanban board.

D. Explain to the compliance department that the control objective is optional because of the use of the agile approach.

114. The lead developer and the quality assurance team member on a scrum team have conflicts that affect the sprint goals following the recent switch to agile. What resolution action should the project manager take?

A. Hold individual meetings with both team members for a resolution to align with the sprint goals.

B. Facilitate a discussion with both team members for a resolution to align with the sprint goals.

C. Evaluate the situation and then educate team members on the effects of their conflicts.

D. Encourage the team members to work together to resolve the conflict and hold a retrospective session to come up with an action plan.

115. Stakeholders are frustrated over the prolonged delivery time of in-house technical services, which was started to reduce costs. What steps should a project manager take to resolve this issue?

A. Replace the in-house team with the contractor who previously provided the service.

B. Collaborate with the stakeholders, understand their concerns and look for ways to reduce delivery time.

C. Add more resources to speed up delivery time.

D. Minimize the delay by asking the team to plan work in parallel.

116. You are the project manager preparing a report on potential delays in a software development project. The report was requested by the project sponsor due to an unforeseen political risk. What tool should you use?

A. Trend Analysis

B. Root Cause Analysis

C. Quality Reports

D. Milestone List

117. A functional manager denies a team member's request for time off compensation. What should the project manager do to guarantee that the team member visits an overseas client site?

A. Confirm with the team member that the client visit

can happen.

B. Negotiate with the team member, the functional manager, and the client to come up with the best possible solution.

C. Log it in the issue log.

D. Confront the functional manager about the time off request.

118. As a project manager, you get a complaint about a previous iteration and its quality metrics reports from a functional manager. The team doesn't feel the complaint is valid. What is the first step you should take?

A. Have a meeting to discuss the functional managers' concerns.

B. Perform a quality audit to validate the applied quality metrics.

C. Review the RACI matrix to identify quality metrics responsibilities.

D. Revise the reports to address the concerns.

119. Near the end of the project, you notice missing technical reports. The team claims they have completed their assigned tasks. What should you do as the project manager?

A. Assign a new team member the task of creating the reports and continuing with the project.

B. Verify roles and responsibilities with the RACI chart.

C. Discuss the activity list with the team and ensure they understand the required work.

D. Review the hierarchical chart in order to confirm relationships and positions.

120. A developer presents unplanned software during the sprint demo, which meets the release date but disrupts priority features for the next two sprints. What can the Scrum team do to minimize the disruption?

A. Collaborate with the product owner on the backlog, the sole input source.

B. Decide independently and present changes during the demo.

C. Approach the Scrum master to discuss the change.

D. Assess the new software and inform the client about the impact on the release plan.

121. The first iteration of a new product was tested in a region but failed to meet the standards in two other regions. What action should the project manager take?

A. Review the results from the first iteration in the retrospective to determine the reasons for non-compliance in the other regions.

B. Ignore the non-compliance issue and launch the product in all regions.

C. Delay the launch in all regions until compliance can be assured.

D. Connect with customers from each region to come to an agreement on the existing design.

122. A team member approaches you as the project manager with concern that some project deliverables may not meet regulatory compliance standards. What action should you take?

A. Schedule a meeting with the key stakeholders and SMEs to get clarity on regulations that can affect project deliverables.

B. Ask for confirmation from the client through an official letter on the applicability of regulations related to project deliverables.

C. Reach out to the PMO to see if the project deliverables are subject to regulations and how to comply.

D. Engage the manager of the team to identify steps to maintain compliance.

123. You are the project manager for an organization that is transitioning to agile approaches in customer projects. What is your role as a servant leader when it comes to a conflict between the development team and product owner over the requirement for legal department approval before shipping releases to the customer? The development team is concerned it can have an impact on the delivery schedule. Also, other departments in the organization don't follow agile practices.

A. Recommend senior managers to implement agile processes across all departments to improve customer satisfaction.

B. Follow established protocols to ensure policies are followed, and risk is minimized.

C. Educate the customer on the organizational procedures and encourage them to tell the leadership.

D. Collaborate with the relevant departments and legal to assess the processes that support project delivery.

124. The company you work for is expanding. As the project manager, what would you prioritize between hiring new resources or outsourcing from an approved vendor team?

A. The expenses of internal resources compared to those from a vendor.

B. The resources of the organization's abilities and

competencies versus those from a vendor.

C. The cost of acquiring services from a local vendor or a global vendor.

D. The companies' procurement practices and guidelines.

125. During the first iteration review of an agile project, there is a request to clarify a monthly report. What should the project manager do?

A. Instruct the project team to prepare a monthly report.

B. Generate a monthly report and give it to the stakeholders.

C. Provide stakeholders with an understanding of agile methodology and its implementation.

D. Ask for the stakeholders to attend a monthly

iteration review.

126. A memo from the project sponsor on a significant initiative calls for an earlier deadline for a critical deliverable. This can potentially impact the original training schedule for a small project team, with a trainer being available as needed. To accommodate the revised timeline milestone, what should the project manager do?

A. Arrange individual training sessions for each member of the project team.

B. Plan a workshop with the trainer for the team, then have several assessment sessions for the internal team.

C. Schedule a series of workshops with the trainer for the team over a shortened timeline.

D. Schedule a dedicated and extended workshop with the trainer for the team before the updated deadline.

127. The project sponsor is frustrated because they are having difficulty understanding the new requirements-gathering process in agile projects since it appears too fast-paced and incomplete. What can the project manager do to address this frustration?

A. Help the project sponsor understand the tools and techniques available and the reason for choosing the current one.

B. Revise the stakeholder register and flag the project sponsor as a potential obstacle.

C. Tell the team about the project sponsor's difficulties and switch from iterative planning to predictive planning.

D. Suspend the project until the scrum master can go over the full backlog with the project sponsor.

128. Amid rapidly changing daily operations and frequent team member turnover in a quickly growing hybrid organization, what can a project manager do to

maintain a stable project?

A. Revise the organizational process assets with the senior leaders' collaboration.

B. Draft a revised team agreement to clarify expectations and responsibilities.

C. Incorporate an update to the team charter to reflect the change in team membership.

D. Review and update the project management plan frequently to address the evolving needs and challenges of the project.

129. After creating the stakeholder list, what should the project manager do next to ensure effective communication with the customer?

A. Hold regular, in-person meetings with both the

customer and stakeholders.

B. Distribute updates to all stakeholders through the best means necessary.

C. Conduct a stakeholder analysis to develop a communications plan.

D. Study past communications with customers and use a similar approach.

130. A team member is showing signs of disengagement during an ongoing project. What can the project manager do to maintain their participation?

A. Have a conversation with the team member to identify the issue and request corrective actions be implemented.

B. Assign a mentor from another team to support the disengaged member.

C. Organize a team meeting to clarify engagement expectations.

D. Encourage the disengaged team member to get additional training to improve their communication abilities.

131. Before the vendor arrives to assist with implementing a new automation process in a factory as a part of an ongoing agile project, what should the project manager do?

A. Turn over critical decisions to the vendor's team to avoid risks.

B. Conduct a briefing to share an understanding of the objectives and expectations of the project among all parties.

C. Provide a communication matrix for team members and the vendor to get familiar with.

D. Emphasize to the project team that the vendor works on behalf of them and that they have the ultimate authority to make decisions.

132. The HR manager hired interns for a project, but their training didn't meet the expected competency-based outcomes. The HR manager refuses to cover the cost of more training since the budget for training has been fully utilized. What can the project manager do to resolve this situation?

A. Formulate training needs for both full-time staff and interns.

B. Identify the gaps in competency and negotiate with the HR manager for alternative options.

C. Communicate hiring and training requirements to the HR manager.

D. Analyze the risk, update the risk register, and inform the HR manager.

133. A senior team member is consistently missing daily stand-up meetings and asking others to provide status updates on their behalf, despite the team adopting agile practices in order to develop an application to meet the needs of the business. What should the project manager do to address this situation?

A. Remind the team member that they need to adhere to the team's working agreement.

B. Let the team handle the working agreement.

C. Replace them with a more reliable team member.

D. Discuss their absence in a meeting with them to explain the impact and find a solution.

134. To enhance team performance by incorporating agile practices in a new project, what method should the project manager adopt?

A. Active listening strategies that cater to the team's needs.

B. Seek funding for the training of team members.

C. Assign a budget for team activities when planning the project.

D. Conduct regular team retrospectives.

135. The client informs the product owner that they want to launch a website a month earlier than planned in order to pursue a business opportunity. What should the project manager instruct the team to do in response to this?

A. Re-plan and adjust the schedule to accommodate the new timeline.

B. Tell the client you can't release the website early.

C. Hold a retrospective meeting to analyze how you can speed up work.

D. Assign additional team members in order to complete the work faster.

136. If team members are unable to concentrate during daily standup meetings because of excessive noise in the workplace, who's accountable for resolving the issue?

A. The Project Manager

B. The Team Members

C. The Stakeholders

D. The Product Owner

137. How can a project manager oversee a risk register and associated risk for a project with the following scenario: The agile team has already created the risk

register through interviews with the stakeholders, workshops, and project charter information?

A. At each spring review session, evaluate and categorize risks.

B. During daily standup meetings, include a discussion of risks.

C. Constantly revise the risk register and review it with the project team.

D. Use iterative risk management to eliminate all risks to the project.

138. You are the project manager on an agile project that is in the first iteration of ten. During the iteration review, the feedback from stakeholders contradicted project objectives. What should you do to address this issue?

A. Encourage the team to meet with the stakeholders to better understand their needs and feedback.

B. Engage the stakeholders to understand their feedback and reconcile it with product backlog refinement.

C. Ask the stakeholders to rank their needs in order of their importance.

D. Ask the project sponsor to clarify the stakeholder's priorities.

139. The project charter is key to ensuring a project team effectively functions. What should the project charter address in regard to the project's objectives and goals?

A. Why the organization gave priority to the project.

B. The main risks and how they will be addressed.

C. Why is the project being done?

D. Who is responsible for the work?

140. During the initial stages of a project, you are the project manager in charge of Team A. You need to collaborate with Teams B, C, and D to launch a complex program. What should be the primary focus for your team?

A. Organizing a team-building activity with representatives from all teams.

B. Implement a dashboard that tracks the metrics of the other teams.

C. Align the priorities of your team with that of the other teams.

D. Encourage all project teams to determine critical dependencies, risks, and milestones.

141. During the iteration retrospective, the team agreed that the reason for working overtime during the last iteration of the agile project was because of a lack of experience in executing assigned tasks. What action should the project manager take?

A. Provide the team with additional training and resources to improve their experience and skills.

B. During the iteration planning session, encourage the team to reassess their effort estimates.

C. Suggest the product owner reassess the product backlog priorities.

D. Submit a change request to the project sponsor for more time in future iterations.

142. An agile project is already underway with a team that has worked together for almost a year when the

customer requests additional features. Considering the requested features are a priority and don't require a lot of additional resources but do require immediate changes in the current iteration, what response should the project manager give?

A. Tell the customer the changes aren't permitted per the agreement.

B. Schedule the request for the start of the next iteration.

C. Collaborate with the team to make the new features a priority and work on the immediate changes needed.

D. Reject the request and explain that incorporating the changes at this stage is a challenge.

143. You are the project manager in a project focused on enhancing a product's market capability. When should be your top priority when defining the key performance indicators or KPIs for the project team?

A. Ensure you can easily measure the KPIs.

B. Align the KPIs with the project objectives and goals.

C. Maximize the performance of the team members.

D. Focus on your personal goals.

144. An agile project was scaled from the feasibility study phase to the implementation phase. The same team was assigned with the exception of one member who was replaced; many team members were unwilling to work with the new member. What should the project manager do to ensure the team is ready to progress to the next phase?

A. Schedule a team-building workshop.

B. Fire the new member.

C. Change the structure of the team.

D. Do nothing, as the team will eventually work together.

145. During a hybrid project Scrum board review, a team member identifies a task that isn't a part of the original project scope but can potentially reduce risk to the project. This task is brought to the team's attention during the review. What is the next step the project manager should take?

A. Analyze the impact of adding the task into the scope and submit a change request if needed.

B. Ask the team to perform a task risk assessment and present the results at the next review meeting.

C. Ask the product owner to evaluate the potential benefits of the task when it comes to meeting the customer's requirements and needs.

D. Include the task backlog to review later.

146. An agile projects team member's overdue user story is causing a delay in a specific functionality and is putting the entire team at risk of missing the goals for the sprint. The reason for the delay is unknown. What is the initial step the project manager should take?

A. Assign a team member to take over the work.

B. Have a discussion with the team member to understand what is causing the delay.

C. Escalate the issue to the project sponsor.

D. Exclude this functionality from the final product.

147. An agile team replaces a key member with a less experienced member. The stakeholder expresses concerns about the project delivery being on time. What steps does the project manager need to take to guarantee successful project completion?

A. Do nothing since the time will adapt to the new member.

B. Replace the new member with a more experienced member.

C. After proper consideration, you chose the new member, so you should proceed with the project as originally planned.

D. Assess the impact, provide proper training, and communicate the project status to the stakeholders.

148. An agile project with a finalized scope and compliance requirements is having a regular review. At this review, the stakeholder informs the project manager of potential changes to the country's safety legislation that may have an impact on the project scope. What should be the project manager's response?

A. Direct the team to proactively initiate changes to the next spring based on the potential new legislation.

B. Assess the potential impact, discuss it with the stakeholders, and determine the best course of action to take.

C. Focus on completing activities based on the product backlog.

D. Have the team wait for the project sponsor to approve an additional budget for the changes to the project scope.

149. The project sponsor requests the conversion of the entire project to an agile approach because of positive results from agile being used on certain parts of the project. What action should the project manager take?

A. Assess the project and its constraints to see if an agile approach is feasible for the entire project and ensure it aligns with the objectives and goals of the company.

B. Submit a change request to the change control board.

C. Work with the project owner to create a product backlog for the entire project.

D. Arrange training for the team to adopt agile.

150. What should the project manager have done to avoid continued support requests and issues with a software program even after administrative closure?

A. Refuse support to end-users after administrative closure.

B. Assign support responsibility to the software development team.

C. Ensure adequate training and documentation are provided to end-users before the software is put into production.

D. Expect end-users to figure the software out on their own.

151. As project manager, you have completed a project charter and received approval from the project sponsor, so you present it to the stakeholders. During the presentation, you notice a low level of engagement from some stakeholders. What is the next step you should take?

A. Add this to the risk register since you are unsure if they understand their role.

B. Arrange individual meetings with the stakeholders to clarify their understanding of key deliverables and responsibilities.

C. Notify the project sponsor of the issue.

D. Assign the team to keep an eye on the stakeholders and track their participation.

152. During a status review of the project with the team, the project manager notices that a vendor resource can finish their work faster than anticipated. Upon reviewing the schedule, the project manager confirms this change and informs the vendor. The vendor disputes the changes and wants the resources to remain for a specified duration. What action should the project manager take?

A. Since the resource needs to stay on, the original schedule should be retained.

B. Confirm the schedule changes and discuss them with relevant people.

C. Start the process of releasing the resources back to the vendor.

D. Review the vendor contract to see if there are clauses regarding resource duration.

153. You are the project manager deploying a new solution across multiple countries. You approve a change in Country A to meet the local customer market requirements. When the changed solution was sent to Country B, it failed to test because of inconsistent regulations. What could have been done to prevent this from happening?

A. You should have canceled the entire deployment and restarted from the beginning.

B. You should have refused the change request for Country A.

C. You should evaluate all change requests related to deployment in each country on a global level before putting them into effect.

D. Testing should have been done before sending the new solution to Country B.

154. Your organization is currently in the middle of a

five-year project, and everything has progressed as planned so far. However, in a recent evaluation the project won't meet a newly implemented international regulation. What should you, as the project manager, do to address this issue and ensure compliance with the new regulation?

A. Organize a meeting with the steering committee to discuss the new regulation and find a solution.

B. Submit a change request.

C. Since the new regulation isn't a part of the initial requirements, you proceed with the project as planned.

D. Ask for funds from the management reserve since the new regulation is an unknown risk.

155. What information does a senior project manager need to get from a junior project manager in order to guide the initiation of the project closure process of an existing project?

A. All planned work is finished successfully, and formal approval is obtained.

B. All project deliverables have been completed and delivered to the customer.

C. All project costs have been charged to the customer.

D. All planned improvements were executed within the approved timeline.

156. A construction company has successfully completed the first phase in a three-year, multi-million dollar stadium rebuild. This phase was completed within the scheduled three-month timeline and budget. What is the next step the project manager needs to take?

A. Advance to the next phase.

B. Get endorsement from the program manager.

C. Start contractual closure procedures for the finished phase.

D. Start the administrative closure procedures.

157. Due to a limited budget, the program manager asks all project managers to prioritize efficiency using the resources available over meeting milestones. The project manager analyzes the resource histogram and discovers that nearly all of the project resources will be utilized in the last month of the project. What are the next steps the project manager should take?

A. Ask for certain tasks to be accelerated to maximize the use of resources.

B. Offer to allocate resources to other projects.

C. Propose that resources are coordinated and balanced across all projects.

D. Stay with the original plan for the project.

158. A new product being developed by your company needs to comply with the necessary non-functional security requirements. The product owner is concerned the team won't be able to implement these requirements effectively. What can you, as the project manager, do to guarantee you'll meet requirements?

A. Have a security expert join the team and review the acceptance criteria for the project.

B. Forward the requirements to the security department for review and implementation.

C. Schedule a discussion to review the requirements during the next sprint meeting.

D. Incorporate the requirements into the project's definition of done.

159. The project sponsor notifies you that a deliverable

created by a contractor is to be given to a nonprofit organization without charge during the close of the project. According to procurement documentation, the contract retains ownership of the deliverable after the contract is completed. What should you, as the project manager, do in response to this situation?

A. Document the lessons learned to register the need for "clear agreement definition during the procurement process."

B. Request a contract change and implement the change control process.

C. Record the transfer as an outstanding issue for the contract department and continue as planned.

D. Review and negotiate the contract to modify ownership of the deliverable.

160. A senior executive is concerned that the project may not be delivering the originally scheduled work

despite key cost parameters showing the project is on track. These concerns were raised in the steering committee meeting. What metrics should the project manager use to address these concerns?

A. Cost Variance

B. Earned Value

C. Schedule Variance

D. Planned Value

161. A team member is frequently absent from team meetings and instead works on tasks assigned by the functional manager. What can be done to address this situation?

A. Schedule a meeting with the team member and their functional manager to discuss the allocation of tasks.

B. Evaluate the impact of their absence and make a decision on whether to reassign them or find other resources.

C. Document their attendance in the performance appraisal.

D. Ask for input from another team member on the issue.

162. You are the project manager for a government organization. You have limited information about the project but know other government organizations have successfully implemented a similar strategy. What estimation method should you use?

A. Parametric Estimation

B. Top-Down Estimation

C. Three-Point Estimation

D. Expert Judgment

163. The customer's project manager resigns at the execution phase of a project, and key stakeholders aren't getting timely updates. What is the next step a project manager should take?

A. Update the communication management plan.

B. Directly notify the primary stakeholders.

C. Keep the project sponsors informed.

D. Send updates until a response is received.

164. You are preparing to meet with the project sponsor after your team members have identified a potential risk during a team meeting. What assessment should you perform in preparation?

A. Qualitative risk analysis

B. Cost-benefit analysis

C. Risk assessment

D. Resource allocation analysis

165. At the initiation stage of a project, the vendor is requested to provide a quote for necessary services. The work was initially estimated at $100,000. As the project advances, requirements are revised to follow the company's procurement procedure and a revised quote is received in excess of $250,000. More than the contingency funds are needed to cover this increased cost. What is the next step the project manager should take?

A. Start a new procurement process and choose another vendor.

B. Negotiate to reduce the cost to the original estimate.

C. Proceed with the best proposal according to the established procurement process.

D. Escalate the concern and involve the steering committee.

166. You are a project manager preparing for an evaluation meeting to address a concern by a key stakeholder claiming the project hasn't achieved the expected business outcomes. What steps should you take to prepare for the meeting?

A. Check the change control log to see if there are approved variations in the project variables.

B. Address the concern by explaining the objectives of the project and the expected outcomes, as well as any misunderstandings.

C. Since work was done according to objectives and goals, carry on with the meeting.

D. Review project data, including project objectives and business case, to understand the perspective of the stakeholder and be able to provide a fact-based response during the meeting.

167. To hold a successful kick-off meeting even though most stakeholders can't attend due to schedule conflicts, what is the best approach?

A. Cancel the meeting and reschedule for when all stakeholders can be present.

B. Proceed with the meeting and hope for the best.

C. Schedule the meeting virtually or as a webinar so stakeholders can participate remotely.

D. Conduct individual meetings with the stakeholders.

168. You are the project manager in the process of

developing the first version of a project management plan for an urban hotel design project with an international, multidisciplinary, and cross-cultural team. What should you do?

A. Consider input from the team members when developing the plan.

B. Conduct a thorough risk assessment before implementing the plan.

C. Separate the project management plan from the risk register because of the complexity of the project, so it is a standalone document.

D. Involve the team and consider cultural differences, then conduct a risk assessment to tailor a plan to your specific project and the team's needs.

169. How can you, as the project manager, guarantee that quality requirements are met while upholding delivery deadlines when you're working with multiple

vendors?

A. Ignore vendor performance as long as products are delivered on time.

B. Document potential impacts of procurement delays in the risk register to reduce the risk of poor quality services and products.

C. Constantly monitor vendor performance and address any deviations to ensure quality and on-time delivery.

D. Assign the procurement process and vendor management to the procurement department since they have the resources and capabilities to handle multiple relationships.

170. You discover that a stakeholder is presenting misleading status reports to the steering committee and needs to get more accurate information on the project. What action should you take?

A. Meet with the stakeholder to understand their view and determine the best action to take.

B. Revise the communication management plan to ensure the stakeholder has access to the needed information.

C. Confront the stakeholder to resolve the issue.

D. Escalate the issue.

171. What method should you use to evaluate the level of stakeholder commitment in a construction project that is 30% complete, as requested by the project sponsor?

A. Ensure the communication management plan is current and relevant.

B. Review the issue log to see what issues have been raised by stakeholders.

C. Interview the stakeholders to assess their commitment level.

D. Check the stakeholder engagement assessment matrix.

172. You receive an email from a stakeholder complaining about work just starting and requesting a change to deliverables in an agile environment; what is the appropriate action to take?

A. Have a meeting with the stakeholder and project owner.

B. Tell the stakeholder that change can't be done in an ongoing sprint.

C. Make the change since they are a key stakeholder.

D. Organize a priority retrospective and invite the stakeholders to participate so you can discuss the requested change during the sprint.

173. The department head is concerned that their requirements are disregarded in the approved management plan while starting a new computerized system. What steps could have been taken to avoid this concern?

A. Involved the department head in the planning process.

B. Set stakeholder expectations.

C. Developed the change management plan to approve change requests.

D. Seek expert input to define project scope.

174. A foreign supplier informs the project manager that the delivery of the last two components for contracted machine production in the factory will only happen if prices are renegotiated. In this situation, what is the first

step the project manager should take?

A. Cancel the supplier's contract.

B. Execute a risk response plan.

C. Explore other sources for the last two components.

D. Have the legal team get involved in the solution.

175. You are in the middle of a project that is 70% complete. A stakeholder raises the issue of additional features that should be added during a review meeting. What should you do next?

A. Assess the impact of the change and perform a backlog refinement.

B. Tell the stakeholder you'll include the changes in future product updates.

C. Incorporate the request into the project plan and notify the correct parties.

D. Submit a change request to the change management board and tell the project sponsor.

176. You are finalizing the exit criteria for a large system development project. You are informed by a risk and compliance stakeholder that a new deliverable related to recent local government legislation must be completed. The change will impact the project's release date. What is your next step?

A. Inform the stakeholder that the new deliverable is outside the scope of the original project plan and a change request needs to be submitted in order to implement the change.

B. Tell the stakeholder that the new deliverable wasn't included in the original exit criteria.

C. Submit a change request to the change control board

for final approval.

D. Have the legal team get involved in the solution.

177. When a project manager is informed that the first in a series of crucial deliveries is delayed and will result in a missed project milestone due to the deliveries being on the critical path, what is the first step to take?

A. Update the schedule and assess the impact on the timeline, budget and quality.

B. Contact the supplier to demand expedited delivery.

C. Update the lesson learned.

D. Register the delay in the issue log.

178. A stakeholder is worried about a project lagging behind because they received unofficial information from team members. After demonstrating to the stakeholders

the latest project status reports, which show the project is still on track with sufficient free floats, what should the project manager do?

A. Draft a memo that project status updates should only go through approved channels.

B. Add the stakeholder to a list of people to receive project updates.

C. Review the communication management plan and make any needed changes.

D. Revamp the status reports and highlight any delays that need corrective action.

179. The development phase of a new product is complete, but the validation test lead is disputing the criteria for an upcoming test. What is the best course of action for a project manager?

A. Investigate the source and determine if a formal change request needs to be submitted to the change control board.

B. Update the test criteria immediately so the test can proceed as planned.

C. Maintain original test criteria to avoid disruption to the project schedule.

D. Clarify the consequences of changing test criteria and persuade the test lead to accept the original criteria.

180. You are newly assigned to a multinational project that is already in progress. You are unfamiliar with the key stakeholders involved. How can you gain an understanding of the stakeholders and the role they play in the project?

A. Review and update the stakeholder register.

B. Conduct a stakeholder analysis to plan effective

communication and engagement strategies.

C. Meet with the resource manager to discuss the stakeholders.

D. Revise the communication plan after determining a communication method.

---

# Answer Key

1. D

2. B

3. A, C and E

4. C

5. B

6. B

7. C

8. C

9. A

10. A

11. D

12. B

13. B

14. A and D

15. C

16. D and E

17. A and C

18. A

19. A

20. D

21. A

22. D and E

23. C

24. D

25. C

26. A

27. B

28. A

29. B

30. C

31. A

32. C and E

33. C

34. B

35. B

36. A and B

37. C

38. C

39. D

40. D

41. B

42. B

43. C

44. C

45. B

46. B

47. B

48. B

49. B

50. D

51. B

52. A

53. B

54. A

55. B

56. A

57. A

58. A

59. B

60. A

61. C

62. C

63. A

64. B

65. B

66. A

67. A

68. B and D

69. A and C

70. A

71. B

72. B

73. C

74. A

75. B

76. A

77. A

78. A

79. B

80. D

81. A

82. B

83. C

84. B

85. C

86. D

87. A

88. C

89. B

90. B

91. C

92. C

93. A

94. A

95. A

96. B

97. B

98. B

99. B

100. A

101. A

102. C

103. C

104. C

105. A

106. C

107. B

108. B

109. A

110. B

111. C

112. B

113. A

114. B

115. B

116. A

117. A

118. C

119. B

120. A

121. A

122. A

123. D

124. B

125. C

126. B

127. A

128. B

129. C

130. A

131. B

132. B

133. D

134. A

135. A

136. A

137. C

138. B

139. C

140. D

141. B

142. C

143. B

144. A

145. A

146. B

147. D

148. B

149. B

150. C

151. B

152. D

153. C

154. B

155. A

156. C

157. C

158. D

159. C

160. C

161. A

162. D

163. A

164. A

165. D

166. D

167. C

168. D

169. C

170. A

171. D

172. A

173. A

174. B

175. A

176. C

177. D

178. C

179. A

180. B